A CULTURAL HISTORY OF RELIGION IN AMERICA

CONTRIBUTIONS TO THE
STUDY OF RELIGION
Series Editor: **Henry W. Bowden**
Private Churches and Public Money: Church-Government Fiscal Relations
Paul J. Weber and Dennis A. Gilbert

A CULTURAL HISTORY OF RELIGION IN AMERICA

JAMES G. MOSELEY

CONTRIBUTIONS TO THE STUDY OF RELIGION, NUMBER 2

GREENWOOD PRESS

WESTPORT, CONNECTICUT • LONDON, ENGLAND

Library of Congress Cataloging in Publication Data

Moseley, James G
    A cultural history of religion in America.

    (Contributions to the study of religion; no. 2
ISSN 0196-7053)
    Bibliography: p.
    Includes index.
    1. United States—Religion. 2. Religion and culture.
I. Title. II. Series.
BL2530.U6M67   200'.973   80-23609
ISBN 0-313-22479-X (lib. bdg.)

Library of Congress Catalog Card Number: 80-23609
ISBN: 0-313-22479-X
ISSN: 0196-7053

First Published in 1981

Greenwood Press
A division of Congressional Information Service, Inc.
88 Post Road West, Westport, Connecticut 06881

Printed in the United States of America

10 9 8 7 6 5 4 3 2 1

For Emily Ann and James Benjamin Moseley

"Neither is new wine put into old wineskins; if it is, the skins burst, and the wine is spilled, and the skins are destroyed; but the new wine is put into fresh wineskins, and so both are preserved." MATTHEW 9:17

CONTENTS

SERIES FOREWORD

Surveys of American religion often treat information with hidden or unexplained methodologies. Sometimes investigations give priority to institutional patterns or to belief systems, and at other times they stress the importance of social or political factors. Authors seldom inform readers about their own viewpoint or how their approach differs from other methods of investigation. One of James Moseley's *A Cultural History of Religion in America*'s many important features is that it brings different methods out into the open and shows how each of them can best be employed.

As a professor of religious studies, Moseley is familiar with different ways of analyzing materials related to belief and behavior. He includes all the major disciplines in this survey without claiming that one is more important than others for a full understanding of the subject. He blends theory and data in each chapter as case studies to demonstrate how various approaches can elucidate religious activity. Without being doctrinaire or prejudicial, he synthesizes perspectives while covering the pertinent facts on mainstream American religious expressions. Such a presentation makes us aware of how different viewpoints enrich our understanding while they open new possibilities for interpreting familiar data with fresh insights.

In addition to providing a case book for showing how different materials can be analyzed, Moseley includes a great deal of information about mainstream American religion. He incorporates all the standard themes into a chronological survey: Puritans, awakenings, revolutionary involvement, camp meetings, belles lettres, ethics, theology, and urban blight and its contemporary challenges. With each setting he shows that a discrete type of inquiry has its own independent strength, able to highlight a specific topic as well as enhance the larger overview. In separate chapters dealing with crucial subjects Moseley applies terms and thought patterns drawn from history of religions, psychology, political analysis, sociological inquiry, religion and literature, ethics, theology, anthropology, and contemporary journalism.

An additional asset is Moseley's clarity. He presents ideas, interpretive schemes, facts, and conclusions with an elegant lucidity that benefits introductory students and specialists alike. Written with rare precision and clarity, the book synthesizes current knowledge of key events germane to American religion. Moseley's style appears simple and uncontrived only because he has spent the time and thought necessary to make it appear artless. This comprehensive survey will serve beginners with accurate information and unconfusing explanations. It will attract more informed readers with a fascinating dexterity.

Religion is a complex phenomenon, and in America its expressions are legion. Moseley builds on that basic observation by adopting a pragmatic attitude, viewing religious studies as a cluster of disciplines in which no single perspective can fully comprehend the variety of data. So this volume succeeds mainly in showing how various modes of investigation apply to many different topics. The method chosen for any chapter could with ingenuity work equally well with topics in each of the book's other chapters. These selected "tunes," as Moseley calls them, challenge readers to create "a new sense of the harmonies" for themselves.

PREFACE

Religion is an aspect of human life. This statement may sound obvious to some and foolish to others. After all, Americans have long distinguished between the "religious" way of doing things and the "secular" approach. Take, for example, the choice of attending a parochial or a public school. One is directly related to a church, the other is not. Yet the values, symbols, and behavior a public school instills often make it appear to be a "church," or perhaps a seminary, of the American way of life. Democracy, independence, and free enterprise are invoked with reverence beyond the merely political. Public education is enshrined—and funded—by Americans as a way to self-fulfillment and social improvement. Even avowedly "secular" institutions sometimes function religiously. Religion cannot be pigeon-holed. Experience has no tidy boundaries.

On the other hand, it *is* foolish to call virtually everything in American life religious in one way or another. Religious experience is a matter of ultimate concern, but that insight is lost when every concern becomes, by extension, somehow "religious." Religion is too important an aspect of human life to be the subject of loose definitional games. One must be more precise. Although there are common elements and continuing undercurrents, different episodes in American life have been religious in fundamentally different ways. One could say that religion has been expressed in different cultural forms at different junctures in our past. No single, overall, vaguely religious perspective will illumine the variousness of religion in America.

Each generation of Americans has produced a new and vital way of being religious. Given the variety of religious developments in American cultural history, no single interpretive perspective will suffice. Understanding the spirit of each episode, and tracing the currents of their influences upon later developments, requires several points of view. For example, insights from psychology of religion may aid in understanding the Great Awakening of the 1740s, whereas literary analysis, sociology, ethical reasoning, or theological reflection may be more appropriate in clarifying later phenomena. Each episode rearranges what has gone before. So while one particular approach may be most helpful for each episode, the overall method must be a principled eclecticism. Such an approach will be useful, too, in a cumulative sense, for making sense of the plurality of spiritual options we have today.

From the press of common experience, in a rapidly spreading American vineyard, each generation has produced its own spiritual wine. While the principal stock has been Protestant Christianity, the vintages have been so various as to require fresh wineskins. An understanding of these wineskins—the cultural forms of religion— is essential for appreciating the developing spirit of American religious history. As a cultural history, then, this volume also serves as an introduction to various methods employed in religious studies.

Such a combination of purposes is appropriate because more limited approaches always miss something of the full life of religion in America. Studies of recognized religious groups usually pay scant attention to the ways religion influences other, distinctly nonchurchly, aspects of American life. For example, a history of American churches would not give much insight into the "civil religion" that some scholars find underpinning, or at times competing with, the churches for the faith of Americans. Neither would such an approach help to illumine the spiritual dimensions of American literature or the religious impulses of the American Revolution. Certainly the churches have played an enormously important role in the history of American culture. But, just as certainly, a more generous perspective is needed to understand the nature of religion in that history.[1] Without claiming to exhaust the resources of each method, or to cover the history in minute detail, I wager that insights from these perspectives will illumine certain interesting events in each episode. An ear for different tunes may initiate a new sense of harmonies. The apparent cacophony may be a "new world" sort of cultural symphony.

The study of religion in America undertaken here proceeds chronologically, rather than topically or thematically. The historical approach is intended to complement, not supercede, the insights of topical and thematic points of view. Readers may wish to pursue further interpretations as proposed later in the epilogue and bibliographic essay, whether by reading more about the history of a particular episode or by investigating certain events from other points of view. Ideally, after studying the primary events and texts upon which the present interpretation is based, the reader will go on to compare religion in America with other cultures and to evaluate various ways of being religious.

Environmentalists teach us to see human life as only one part of a vast, intricate, interacting network of natural resources. It may be helpful, in analogous fashion, to think of America as a cultural ecosphere. Just as human life plays a significant role in the natural world, so religion is a vitally important aspect of the cultural system. As George Santayana put it: "You may disregard your environment, you cannot escape it; and your disregard of it will bring you moral empoverishment and some day unpleasant surprises."[2] The best way to avoid such costly surprises, in the cultural as in the natural world, is to acquire a sense of one's place in a living tradition.

Thanks to a Fellowship in Residence for College Teachers from the National Endowment for the Humanities, much of the research and initial writing of this book was accomplished during a seminar on "Religion and Modernity: The American Case," led by John F. Wilson at Princeton University. While I have learned from many people in writing this book, I want especially to acknowledge the helpful criticism and suggestions given by my friend Rowland A. Sherrill and by my colleague Justus D. Doenecke and three others—John P. Diggins, Martin E. Marty, and John F. Wilson— who read the manuscript in its entirety. Helen Davidson deserves thankful recognition for her intelligent, accurate typing of the final manuscript. My intellectual debts, as you will see on reading the book, are too various for a simple accounting. I hope to make them good by using the ideas so widely gained to tell an important story in a new way. Of course I own whatever mistakes my telling involves, hoping only to discount them to the enthusiasm of an ambitious project.

NOTES

1. See the review by Robert S. Michaelson of Robert T. Handy's *A History of the Churches in the United States and Canada* in *Religious Studies Review* 4, no. 2 (April 1978): 101-4; and the review by John F. Wilson of some reviews of Sydney E. Ahlstrom's *A Religious History of the American People* in *Religious Studies Review* 1, no. 1 (September 1975): 1-8.

2. George Santayana, *Character and Opinion in the United States* (New York: W. W. Norton and Company, Inc., 1967), p. 229.

A CULTURAL
HISTORY
OF RELIGION
IN AMERICA

1

AMERICAN PURITANISM AND THE HISTORY OF RELIGIONS

Why do the Puritans—only a handful of early settlers—exercise such a strong hold on America's remembrance? After all, New England was only one section of the American colonies, and, even in the Massachusetts Bay Colony, church-going Puritans composed no more than 20 percent of the population. Yet this minority wielded great influence throughout the seventeenth century, on later generations of Americans, and on the thinking of historians. In part, the Puritans were influential because their main settlement, the Bay Colony, was one of the earliest and most successful colonies in the New World. Also, they were well educated and had an elaborately articulated sense of identity and purpose. But it is primarily in terms of religion that we remember the Puritans. We must dig deeper to understand why subsequent generations accorded the Puritans so large a share in establishing the meaning of religion in America.

The Puritans had a highly coherent, theologically ordered sense of themselves, their role in history, and the meaning of their settlement in the New World. Such cultural coherence and religious assurance are things most Americans have wanted. Yet, influential as they were, much about the Puritans seems curiously remote from modern consciousness. Rather than evaluating the Puritans by later religious developments, it may be well to adopt an archaic point of view. The core of the Puritan experience, as well as the substance of their influence, may be better understood if we consider the nature of religion itself in human history.

Max Weber and Emile Durkheim have observed that any social group possesses a core of common values. These values integrate various aspects of life and are anchored to ultimate reality by religious perceptions and beliefs. Such an observation liberates the study of religion from a Western theological framework and from being pursued primarily in the service of Christian institutions. Even as modern Christendom incurs charges of social irrelevance and intellectual confusion, many religious scholars are finding fresh resources by investigating values from other places and times. If modern Western religion has become full of uncertainties and contradictions, the religiousness of primitive peoples appears increasingly clear. Despite technical differences, many cultural anthropologists and historians argue that the religions of archaic peoples are somehow purer or more unified than our own.

Mircea Eliade, a leading scholar of the history of religions, interprets archaic man's experience as sharply divided between "sacred" and "profane" spheres. In religious myths and rituals, contact with sacred powers relieves the tedium of everyday, ordinary existence. In each culture, certain manifestations of the sacred, Eliade maintains, enable primitive people to discover meaning and order in life. These manifestations or hierophanies, such as a cosmic tree or a god of the sky, thus save primitive peoples from the spiritual death which follows from overexposure to the relentless drone of profane time and the uninterrupted banality of profane space. Symbolically expressed in myths and rituals, hierophanies give primitive men and women continuing access to the power of sacred reality, thus enabling their personal and social experience to be integrated or culturally holistic. Likewise, the religious unity of American Puritanism is seen in John Cotton's remark in 1636 to Lord Say and Seal that "the word, and scriptures of God doe conteyne a short *upoluposis*, or platforme, not onely of theology, but also of other sacred sciences, . . . attendants, and handmaids thereunto . . . ethicks, eoconomicks, politicks, church-government, prophecy, academy."[1] Evidently the religiously integrated quality of primitive life is more than a relic of prehistoric times.

Earlier students of primitive societies tended to romanticize such unified, holistic religion, setting it in stark opposition to the secularization, dislocation, and general chaos found in modern society. Indeed, the terms primitive and modern, despite protestations to the contrary, imply sharp distinctions and suggest that human history shows either marked progress toward rational enlightenment or a lamentable decline in religiousness. Recently, anthropologists such as Mary Douglas have uncovered evidence indicating that there need not be a straight line of development from primitive to advanced societies. Some so-called archaic or traditional peoples apparently have been quite as rational and secular in their outlook on life as modern people are generally supposed to be. And the religious myths and rituals of many modern people sometimes seem quite primitive. Evidently there is no iron-clad logic or empirical justification for an evolutionary cultural perspective.

Although no direct line of progress may be seen, there are real differences between peoples whose religious experience is holistic and those whose religion is separate from other aspects of their lives. To maintain the validity of the insights of Eliade and other scholars into the phenomena of religion, we need to replace an overworked differentiation between primitive and modern religions with a more useful distinction between what we may call concentric and free-floating ways of being religious. Many early societies foster a concentric cultural orientation, with religious experience and symbols at the center of social, economic, and political affairs. The cultures of most later societies become increasingly free-floating, with religion simply one part of life alongside others. American history has moved from primarily concentric toward more free-floating ways of being religious. Pursuing this distinction clarifies both American Puritanism and the special character of its contributions to American history.

Among tribal or otherwise hierarchically organized cultures, a religious view of life is the core of both individual and social identity. Religion provides a shared apprehension of or attitude toward life as grounded in and bounded by a sacred reality which transcends and supports the human and secures its ultimate meaning and worth. However broadly the sacred reality is symbolized, generally stable social conditions support a sense of life as unified and coherently ordered through religion. Religious values, perceptions, and beliefs appear at the very center of life itself. Life's otherwise disparate dimensions—economic, political, psychological, social, artistic—are rendered congruent by religion. As John Cotton put it, "Gods institutions (such as the government of church and commonwealth be) may be close and compact, and co-ordinate one to another, and yet not be confounded."[2]

It is not a matter of everything becoming somehow religious. It is, rather, a particular manifestation of the sacred, revealing unbreakable bonds between an individual's kinship, occupation, social history, and the natural world and the basic order of reality itself. In Cotton's words, "Gods all-sufficient wisdome" and "the fulnes and perfection of Holy Scriptures" not only "prescribe perfect rules for the right ordering of a private mans soule to everlasting blessednes with himselfe, but also for the right ordering of a mans family, yea, of the commonwealth too, so farre as both of them are subordinate to spiritual ends."[3] The tremendous power of religious symbols is shown in the way they embody and express a coherent sense of all of life's activities. For such a group, religion is the heart of every meaningful experience. With the sacred at the center, life's dimensions are experienced—and symbolized—as concentric.

Religion does not always assume a concentric orientation. For individuals undergoing social change, life does not seem holistic or, in some cases, ordered in any meaningful way. For such people, various aspects of life are often unrelated; religious values and symbols eventually exist alongside political, economic, and other conditions. A person's center of significance may shift from aspect to aspect as he or she lives through changing situations. Different people may develop increasingly personal and private ways of ordering their experiences. For some, religion may be all-important; others may find religious symbols powerful only occasionally, or not at all. Later we will investigate free-floating ways of being religious. For the moment, let us examine the substance of the Puritans' remarkably concentric way of being religious.

Increasingly frustrated in their attempts in the sixteenth and seventeenth centuries to reform the Church of England, a band of "Puritans"—as their opponents disparagingly called them—departed for New England. While most Puritans remained in England, the people who came to the New World saw themselves as the shock troops of a Calvinist internationale. Their goal was to establish a "citty vpon a hill," and thereby show the world, especially Englishmen, how a holy commonwealth ought to be ordered. Perry Miller, the preeminent scholar of Puritanism in America, shows how their adventure shifted direction. Perhaps no other group of immigrants, except the Israelites, whom the Puritans so often adopted as models, has known so emphatically what its migration was supposed to accomplish. Yet almost from the outset, leading voices among them began to lament a change of meaning, a loss of purpose. The new land and its "salvage" inhabitants made the going rough, but the early Puritans persevered and, before long, began to prosper. Then why was the self-accusing "jeremiad" their most characteristic form of sermon? What happened to make their spokesmen so disappointed?

Miller has shown how the Puritans soon lost their sense of enacting their drama on a world stage. The English civil war made the "citty" upon a Massachusetts hill seem remote or irrelevant to most Englishmen. Being, as it were, their own audience, the Puritans were, in Miller's fine phrase, "left alone with America." The nature of their "errand into the wilderness" underwent a subtle yet profound alteration. Although they continued to watch England carefully, the running of their errand now became more immediately significant than its original international purpose. Without an English church to reform or an English society to reconstruct, the Puritans were free to create a biblical, God-ordained church and state in their New World. Instead of feeling a sense of liberation, though, they began to worry lest their remarkably concentric view of life begin to become unglued, as, to their fascinated consternation, it very soon did. All sorts of unanticipated problems arose. Yet, since the Puritans were first and foremost a religious people, they expressed their concerns primarily in theological terms. Theology was the mode in which they reflected upon and came to terms with challenges, boons, and dilemmas of all sorts.

The Puritans had hoped to establish "a due form of government,

both civill and ecclesiastical" and to construct, nurture, and maintain a society commensurate with the covenant they believed
existed between themselves and God. As John Cotton explained:

> It is better that the commonwealth be fashioned to the setting forth
> of Gods house, which is his church: than to accomodate the church
> frame to the civill state. Democracy, I do not conceyve that ever
> God did ordeyne as a fitt government eyther for church or common-
> wealth. If the people be governors, who shall be governed? As for
> monarchy, and aristocracy, they are both of them clearly approoved,
> and directed in scripture, yet so as referreth the soveraigntie to
> himselfe, and setteth up Theocracy in both, as the best form of
> government in the commonwealth, as well as in the church.[4]

For the Puritans religion was the vital center of a corporate,
social enterprise. "Seeing the church is to determine who shall be
members, and none but a member may have to doe in the government of a commonwealth," John Cotton attempted to explain to
the skeptical Lord Say and Seal that "magistrates are neyther
chosen to office in the church, nor doe governe by directions from
the church, but by civill lawes" as enacted and executed in general
courts of justice. "In all which," Cotton claimed, "the church (as
the church) hath nothing to doe: Onely," as he forthrightly concluded, "it prepareth fitt instruments both to rule, and to choose
rulers, which is no ambition in the church, nor dishonor to the
commonwealth."[5] For at least a century, political, economic,
literary, and social affairs reflected the Puritans' central religious
convictions. But subsequent developments in these other areas began to pull hard at the pattern they wanted to weave. And, as Miller has suggested, there were some loose threads in the center of the
Puritan theological design.

Most Puritan divines took their cues from John Calvin, but ordinary people found little comfort in Reformed doctrines of pre-
destination and double damnation. Since no one in this life knows
with full certainty if he or she has been "elected" by grace to be one
of the "saints," God's absolute transcendence may seem so fearful
as to enervate even the most sincere believers. Hence early Puritan
spokesmen found solace in the idea of a covenant—a freely given,
unbreakable bond of mutual support—between God and his

people. Although it was at best a minor theme in Calvin's thought, this "federal" theology developed by English Puritans like William Ames became a staple of religious thought in the New World. Intended as a source of peace for troubled consciences, the notion of a covenant relation between God and men may, in certain circumstances, be interpreted almost as a contract. As the English Puritan theologian John Preston put it, "You may sue him of his own bond written and sealed, and he cannot deny it."[6] Despite intense efforts to sustain a sense of the transcendent sovereignty of God, the American Puritans felt increasingly in full control of their lives. So the covenant, instead of being the last hope of sinners, might be construed as a basis for negotiating with a divine, but increasingly equal, partner. Political and commercial affairs seemed less and less under the control of the Almighty. The human agents of God's will began to seem as important as the sovereign authority they set out to serve.

Challenges to their understanding of a communally convenanted social order rippled outward from the crucial, finally unstable ambiguities in the Puritans' sense of religious selfhood. On the one hand, they believed that individuals can accomplish nothing toward their own salvation. All have sinned, and each stands in jeopardy of eternal damnation, saved only by the unmerited, freely given grace of God. On the other hand, the intensity of such a psychic drama calls attention continually to the self. Controversies began about whether and to what extent one should prepare oneself for grace. Surely, if a person has done all that may be expected, is not God bound to save? John Calvin, their tough-minded theological mentor, would have told them plainly, no. But in the New World, circumstances were such that the tensions in the Puritan idea of selfhood were rarely, or only temporarily, resolved.

As early as 1636, the "Antinomian crisis" demonstrated how a theological imbalance could threaten the coherence of the Puritan social order. When Mistress Anne Hutchinson spoke of new, direct communication with God, the established clergy was in an uproar. "The differences in the said points of religion increased more and more, and the ministers of both sides," observed Governor John Winthrop on 20 January 1637, "did publicly declare their judgments in some of them, so as all men's mouths were full of them."[7]

In some ways, Hutchinson's extreme reliance on personal revelation came straight from the heart of the Puritan doctrine of salvation. This won her the initial support of John Cotton. But if the Holy Ghost dwells in the hearts of all the regenerate, why should ministers be accorded any special spiritual authority? If all followed their own intuitions, what chaos might not ensue? As Governor Winthrop noted:

> Every occasion increased the contention, and caused great alienation of minds; and the members of Boston (frequenting the lectures of other ministers) did make much disturbance by public questions, and objections to their doctrines, which did in any way disagree from their opinions; and it began to be as common here to distinguish between men, by being under a covenant of grace or a covenant of works, as in other countries between Protestants and papists.[8]

The answer was clear, even to Cotton: toleration of such spiritual intoxication would undermine the integrity of the entire Puritan errand. Banishment, however, was only a temporary solution. Such tensions were inherent in the Puritan system. Changing social conditions might allow even more widespread outbursts of enthusiasm in the future, as in the 1650s when the Puritan hierarchy was confronted by the Quakers. Intense efforts notwithstanding, the Puritan synthesis—of individual and of community, and of individual-in-community—began to crack.

The disruption of Puritan religious life can be understood when we consider the forces influencing its periphery. Since their culture was holistic, changes in one area of life soon disturbed the balance of the whole. Economic demands and successes exacerbated the strains at the religious heart of American Puritanism. It was difficult for any but the staunchest to remain fully committed. Prosperity made it hard for the second and, especially, third generations honestly to "own" the covenant that had sustained their elders through the dangers of migration and rigors of settlement. After deep searchings of heart and long theological arguments, a "Half-Way Covenant" (even the name is ironic) was established as early as 1662. This strange instrument granted church membership, but not Holy Communion, to offspring of the original "saints," without requiring their public testimony to an inner experience of grace.

With the Half-Way Covenant, the Puritan sense of sacred time—the idea of their history as full of divine purpose—lost its certainty. The continuity was still affirmed, but the affirmations began to sound forced. What had happened to work such havoc?

As the community of saints disintegrated from within, the number of recognized Puritans become an ever smaller minority in the Bay Colony. The Puritans had never been—or thought of themselves as being—a numerical majority. As increasing numbers of non-Puritan immigrants continued to arrive, however, the Puritans could hope to remain in control only by wielding religious symbols with understood social and political power. For example, observance of the Sabbath, the community-wide ritual for consecrating weekly time, was enforced by fines, physical punishment, and social censure. But it was difficult to maintain the coherence of these religious symbols, and the swelling non-Puritan population made the Puritans' social authority precarious. Other nonreligious developments, such as the triumph of the latter Stuarts in England and the revocation of the Massachusetts Bay Charter, undercut the political power of Puritan religious symbols even more.

From the outset, the Puritans feared the consequences of economic success with a passion equal to the energy they had put into building their settlements and securing their gains. As Max Weber's analysis of earlier European Calvinists suggests, the intensity of the Puritans' religious convictions fueled economic engines that operated, in turn, to weaken the hold of religion on the people's lives. In 1662, a year of great drought as well as the spiritual aridity of the Half-Way Covenant, poet Michael Wigglesworth adopted the voice of the Lord, in "God's Controversy with New-England," to ask:

Whence cometh it, that Pride, and Luxurie
    Debate, Deceit, Contention, and Strife,
False-dealing, Covetousness, Hypocrisie
    (With such like Crimes) amongst them are so rife,
That one of them doth over-reach another?
    And that an honest man can hardly trust his Brother?

How is it, that Security, and Sloth,
    Amongst the best are Common to be found?

> That grosser sins, in stead of Graces growth,
>   Amongst the many more and more abound?
> I hate dissembling shews of Holiness.
>   Or practice as you talk, or never more profess.[9]

With continuing economic success, a merchant elite began to supplant the clergy's social power and symbolic prestige. Instead of a holy commonwealth, Boston was fast becoming a trading center, linking the New World with the Old. Ministers had to pay heed to the wishes of a growing commercial aristocracy. While some continued to challenge economic interests, ministers were increasingly tempted to cater to the new prosperity. Success in one sphere spelled doom in another. The once preeminently powerful clergy now spoke with full authority to only one, increasingly private aspect of people's lives.

The Puritans had hoped to establish and protect the hierarchical social structure they had inherited from England. In 1630, "On Boarde the Arrabella, On the Attlantick Ocean," John Winthrop delivered "A Modell of Christian Charity" as a lay-sermon to the passengers, supporting with reasons and scripture proofs the proposition that

> GOD ALMIGHTIE in his most holy and wise providence hath soe disposed the Condicion of mankinde, as in all times some must be rich some poore, some highe and eminent in power and dignitie; others meane and in subieccion.[10]

But by the 1680s, the concept of "the godly ruler" was fading, as the religious legitimization of political and social order gave way to a rhetoric of property rights. The new prosperity was dissolving Winthrop's stratified view of society, and undermining its religious foundations. John Cotton had believed that "Purity, preserved in the church, will preserve well ordered liberty in the people, and both of them establish well-ballanced authority in the magistrates."[11] But social change and increasingly free-floating religious symbols were two sides of the same American coin.

In addition, land distribution was a major problem. Instead of primogeniture, it was the Puritans' practice to divide their worldly estates equally among their sons. This led, as children multiplied, to a scarcity of land within established towns. Some of the heirs were forced to move into new towns, where resources were more abundant. This dispersal of the population diffused the cultural hegemony of the original settlement. Parts of the wilderness were tamed into towns. New towns needed new covenants; the spread of the people weakened the notion of a unitary, purposeful Puritan errand. New settlements drained the spiritual authority of the original sacred spaces; if all of the New World was potentially hierophanic, religious diversity was bound to ensue. Demographic variations and economic success had combined to weaken the social power of a set of religious symbols already on the brink of dissolution. Religious affairs were still tremendously important in New England life, but spiritual concerns were less at the center of most people's public lives. Although religious symbols and values were still present—perhaps even predominant—in the culture, the arrangement was no longer concentric. Religion became one element in a more fluid social system.

Given the theological and social strains at work in the "citty vpon a hill," it might seem that Puritanism would be of little direct consequence to later generations of Americans. Some of the elements of the Puritan synthesis became significant undercurrents in American life. Their concern for purity in the public order and their desire for the inward working of divine grace, for example, were renewed at critical moments in the nation's subsequent history. As historian David Leverenz says, "a preoccupation with things spiritual as well as material, a concern with group betterment rather than individual success, a preoccupation with mastering one's self as well as one's environment: these aspects remained, long after a provincial tradesman's world had split the Puritan experiment into its disparate elements."[12] Beyond the influence of these undercurrents, our earlier discussion of the history of religions and, especially, our distinction between concentric and free-floating ways of being religious suggest the major role of Puritanism in American cultural history.

The Puritans, however briefly, had a concentric arrangement of symbols and values that were dispersed loosely throughout the colonies and through much of America's history. In addition to increasing the impact of Puritan elements on later episodes of

American life, the remembered coherence of Puritan religion functions as a ideal for envisioning and assessing subsequent ways of being religious.[13] Later Americans praised their religious forefathers and envied—or emulated—their spiritually unified lives. The concentric order of Puritan life thus has an influence beyond the range of specific Puritan theological ideas and spiritual practices. The Puritan ideal enlivened the religious vision of Americans for generations. The thoroughly religious integration of Puritan life also serves as a holistic ideal for imagining American futures.

If we are, as historian Sydney Ahlstrom has said, at the end of "the Puritan era," it is not because we are beyond the influence of their ideas and symbols. These recur and reach the present. Rather, we think of contemporary America as post-Puritan because we have become inescapably aware of our ethnic, religious, and cultural pluralism. Various aspects of our lives freely shift in importance and change in significance. Hence the spiritual coherence Americans still seek cannot be the kind the Puritans had. Perhaps we can best honor the integrity of the Puritan spirit by leaving their ideal behind and seeking to realize our own. Gaining such religious independence is, in an interesting and important way, what the Puritan errand was all about.

NOTES

1. Perry Miller and Thomas H. Johnson, eds., *The Puritans: A Sourcebook of Their Writings*, 2 vols. (New York: Harper and Row, 1963) 1:209.

2. Ibid.

3. Ibid.

4. Ibid., 1:209-10.

5. Ibid., 1:210.

6. Cited in Perry Miller, *Errand Into the Wilderness* (New York: Harper and Row, 1956), p. 72.

7. Quoted in Miller and Johnson, eds., *The Puritans*, 1:131.

8. Ibid., 1:132.

9. Ibid., 2: 613.

10. Ibid., 1: 195.

11. Ibid., 1: 212.

12. David Leverenz, *The Language of Puritan Feeling: An Exploration in Literature, Psychology, and Social History* (New Brunswick: Rutgers University Press, 1980). p. 137.

13. Sacvan Bercovitch has recently underscored the Puritans' own emphasis on progress toward a new future. See pp. 65-68 of his "Rhetoric and History in New England: The Puritan Errand Reassessed," in Louis J. Budd, Edwin H. Cady, and Carl L. Anderson, eds., *Toward a New Literary History: Essays in honor of Arlin Turner* (Durham, N.C.: Duke University Press, 1980), pp. 54-68. Bercovitch reinterprets Puritanism more fully in his *The American Jeremiad* (Madison, Wisc.: University of Wisconsin Press, 1978).

2

THE GREAT AWAKENING AND THE PSYCHOLOGY OF RELIGION

Unlike the "citty vpon a hill" envisioned by the Puritans, eighteenth-century New England was fast becoming a "bustling provincial society" which was "free, individualistic, democratic" and "Western but not European."[1] As early settlements grew into prosperous towns and commercial cities, their religious institutions became more conservative. Religious affiliations provided social identity for people living in an increasingly complex culture. As Puritan religious symbols became more free-floating, individual piety was often prey to secular social, political, and economic concerns. Religion no longer seemed a natural aspect of life. Many Puritans became "puritanical," searching their hearts and moralistically blaming their times for the lack of religious zeal. Lamentations over the decline of true religion became so conventional as to gain the status of a distinctive literary and homiletic genre—the "jeremiad"—and no longer stirred desires for renewal. Such tendencies vexed many believers and led traditional divines to despair.

Yet the inward, personal power of Puritan spirituality was too fecund to lie dormant for long. In the 1730s, surprising events began to express the needs of the people for vital religious experience. A lively frontier revival spread through the Connecticut River Valley, and soon a "great and general Awakening" was under way

throughout the colonies. The Great Awakening was a complex social phenomenon with important political consequences. But to
people caught up in the revivals themselves, the Awakening was
primarily a matter of inward religious experience. For many Americans, the most pressing issue of life was whether one had been
spiritually reborn.

Heated theological controversies soon arose. The perspicacious
"participant-observer" Jonathan Edwards gave the most trenchant
analysis of the "wonderful works" of the spirit. But his careful interpretations came in theological treatises which now seem remote.
Edwards's thinking is a prime resource, yet our cultural analysis of
the Awakening may best begin with historian Richard L. Bushman's clue that "a psychological earthquake had reshaped the human landscape."[2] Modern developments in the psychological
sciences may reveal the inward religious meanings and suggest the
cultural significance of this important episode in American history.

Religion is difficult to comprehend neatly because its concerns
are cosmic and its imperatives may touch all aspects of social life.
Also, much of what many people consider the heart of religion is
inescapably personal and hence may frustrate objective investi-
gators. Until recently, "states of the soul," those internal experiences composing so much of the life of religion, were described
only in language from sacred scriptures and portrayed only according to accepted patterns of churchly mythology. Analysis of such
phenomena proceeded within the guidelines of established theological frameworks. When mystical reveries transcended traditional meditative programs, or when "heretical" speculations trans-
gressed normal theological bounds, such "excesses" had to rely
upon—even when most vehemently denying—the formulations of
an explicitly religious realm of existence and reflection. Religious
experience, however meaningful for believers, was a closed book
for anyone outside the community of faith.

Mystical flights may never be fully appreciated by uninterested
spectators. But one can be sympathetic without becoming directly
involved. The rise of the psychological sciences in the twentieth
century has made possible the interpretation of inward religious experiences in nonecclesiastical and nontheological terms. A psychological perspective need not be reductionistic; the attempt is not to

explain religion away by exchanging theological for other, supposedly more scientific labels. Rather, an adequate psychology of religion should interpret spiritual phenomena in ways that are at once faithful to the actual experience of believers and also comprehensible to people without religious presuppositions. A psychological approach to religion is not simply a therapeutic tool. It has many nonclinical uses: it may increase understanding in the service of belief, or enrich human relationships, or give experiential ballast to theological speculations. A properly elaborated psychology should help us understand the behavior and beliefs of people whose religious experiences we may not share. So psychology can be a powerful aid in the study of religion in history. In this light, what insights from the psychology of religion help us to interpret the Great Awakening?

Sigmund Freud was, of course, the first to articulate those distinctions between aspects of the self—the ego, the id, and the superego—so critical to the understanding of psychological disorders. Freud saw religion as a symptom of an incomplete or pathological person. He interpreted God as the projection of human father figures and believed that psychoanalysis could liberate people from the "illusion" of religion. While his observations are useful in studying religion, many religious people feel that a Freudian perspective violates rather than clarifies their most important experiences. Carl Jung, initially a student and colleague of Freud's, pressed beyond the ideas of his teacher to adumbrate the collective undercurrents of conscious selfhood. Although Jung has much to say about how the "archetype of rebirth" contributes to the process of individuation, William James provides the most direct resources for a psychological interpretation of the Great Awakening. James's psychology is more tentative than many, but he was hard-headed (like Freud) and also took religion very seriously (like Jung). His American background made James keenly aware of concerns that had exercised the theological imagination of Jonathan Edwards.

William James first academic work was in psychology. As his physiological investigations led into philosophical questions, he became increasingly interested in religion. Many of his essays explore such religious issues as the freedom of the will and the nature of the universe. He also was a leader in modern scientific efforts to examine psychic phenomena. When James was invited to deliver the prestigious Gifford Lectures in Scotland, he undertook a psychological investigation of "the varieties of religious experience."

After hearing spiritual case histories and colorful excerpts from lives of religious exuberance, James's audience must have found his conclusions deceptively simple. There is "a certain uniform deliverance in which all religions appear to meet," said James, which consists of two parts: first, an uneasiness, "a sense that there is *something wrong about us* as we naturally stand"; and then its solution, "a sense that *we are saved from the wrongness* by making proper connection with the higher powers."[3] In the process of such deliverance, James emphasizes, a person begins to identify his "real" being with a "higher" part of himself, becoming:

> *conscious that this higher part is conterminous and continuous with a MORE of the same quality, which is operative in the universe outside of him, and which he can keep in working touch with, and in a fashion get on board of and save himself when all his lower being has gone to pieces in the wreck.*[4]

Contact with the "more" beyond human experience takes a variety of individual and cultural forms, and the "more" itself is symbolized in many ways. James hypothesized that "whatever it may be on its farther side, the 'more' with which in religious experience we feel ourselves connected, is on its *hither* side the subconscious continuation of our conscious life."[5] For James the subconscious provides a "subliminal door" to sources of illumination and spiritual energy far beyond the confines of the everyday, waking self.

If James was personally a "healthy-minded" moral optimist, he found the regenerative passage of the "sick soul" by far the more profound spiritual course. A pattern of rebirth emerges from the wide range of James's colorful examples. The "divided soul" moves—suddenly or gradually, willfully or by self-surrender—toward a religious unification through regeneration. However else they are evaluated, and James was constitutionally averse to systematic theology, these experiences yield fruits which everyone recognizes as characteristic of "saintly" lives: asceticism, strength of soul, purity, and charity.[6] James insists that the process of conversion which generates such undeniable virtues cannot be understood by splitting the soul into categories or faculties. Actual experience, whether religious or not, is an integral whole. We may speak abstractly of subjective and objective aspects, but a "full fact," a "concrete bit of personal experience" includes "a conscious field *plus* its object as felt or thought of *plus* an attitude towards the object *plus* the sense of a self to whom the attitude belongs."[7] Spiritual states may be analyzed psychologically, but James warns against "scientific" explanations that oversimplify the complex integrity of actual experience.

If anyone ever tried to be true to the wholeness of actual experience, and championed the regenerative religiousness of the "twice-born" over the moralism of the "once-born" (to stick with James's terms), that person was Jonathan Edwards. Some of his language—"Providence," "depravity," "efficacious grace"—now sounds antique. But William James's observations will help us understand Edwards's theology. The Great Awakening was complex and confusing even for Edwards's contemporaries. But James's psychological investigations of religious experience frame the proper questions and suggest the clarity of Edwards's answers.

We might approach the Great Awakening by asking whether the people involved experienced what James called a sense of uneasiness about themselves and, if so, through what process of deliverance its solution came. The widespread preoccupation with sin and salvation, the frequent outbursts of emotion, and the lively and prolonged religious controversies of the time indicate pervasive spiritual unrest. Unstable political conditions, rapidly changing social expectations, and unresolved ambiguities in the sense of selfhood (inherited from their Puritan founders) heightened the religious restlessness of many eighteenth-century Americans. To see how these cultural factors influenced the consciousness of the Great Awakening, we should follow historian George Bancroft's advice: "He that would know the workings of the New England mind in the middle of the [eighteenth] century, and the throbbings of its heart, must give his days and nights to the study of Jonathan Edwards."[8]

The frontier revival of the 1730s began in Northhampton as Edwards was preaching a series of sermons on justification by faith.

Edwards attributed these fresh outpourings of the spirit to the salutary effects of sound Reformed doctrines. As the spirit continued to move, proponents and detractors of the revival began to argue in earnest. Edwards asked the basic question: what is true religion? Edwards pursued this question so persistently that, as philosopher John E. Smith says, the soul's relation to God is the key issue of Edwards's writings, and of the entire Awakening as well.[9] Edwards's analysis shows that he was considerably more complex than his frequent textbook caricature—the preacher of the Enfield sermon, "Sinners in the Hands of an Angry God." Probing the soul's relation to God, Edwards formulated what today we might call a theological psychology. He worked out his thinking in narratives, treatises, and dissertations responding to the drama of the revival and the "great and general Awakening." These writings are valuable both theologically and as an interpretation of the religious events of his time. To enter the world of Edwards's thought, we need to follow the serial progress of his works.

In the "Personal Narrative" of his early spiritual experiences, as in his *A Faithful Narrative of the Surprising Work of God in the Conversion of Many Hundred Souls*, *The Distinguishing Marks of a Work of the Spirit of God*, and *Some Thoughts Concerning the Present Revival of Religion in New England*, Edwards describes and documents the soul's experience of God. He argues that experience, not theological ideas or moral practice, is the central matter of religion. Yet he also recognizes that not all moving or seemingly profound experiences are truly religious. So he proceeds to "test the spirits," and this first phase of his mature thinking culminates in *A Treatise Concerning Religious Affections*. He enumerates feelings, such as a peculiar intensity or certain sequence of emotions, which are not necessarily works of God. And he discusses those experiences that believers should interpret as signs of true religion. His central point is that God saves by creating a "new sense" in a person's heart; no one can manufacture, however subtly or sincerely, true religious affections. Echoing John Calvin, Edwards maintains that only through the operation of divine grace does a sense of God's holiness, majesty, justice, and beauty arise within a person. The center of such a sense is delight in the glory of God, Himself, rather than any benefits—including salvation—one might hope to gain by being religious. Only this realization can produce a life of actual piety, and such a life, rather than "religious" assertions, moral heroics, or strange sensations, is the best evidence of authentic regeneration.

The bare outline of such ideas suggests how Edwards's convictions got him into trouble when, a decade later, the flames of the Awakening began to diminish. For Edwards was convinced that only someone with a new sense of the heart was a true "saint," and that everyone else—for their own good, lest their hypocrisy lead to eternal damnation—should be excluded from the communion of the faithful. Because prosperity and spirituality were at war, Edwards lost his church and, with his wife and seven children, went to minister to the frontiersmen and Indians at Stockbridge. In this new post, he continued undaunted to develop and refine his thinking.

Next Edwards argued that God's salvation comes to the whole person. He made this point by showing that an individual's spiritual existence requires more than good intentions and will power. Unwilling to compromise God's majesty, Edwards challenged a group of theologians who agreed with Jacob Arminius that salvation depends to some extent on the free action of human will. Edwards was arguing against a cluster of popular notions called Arminianism—"a loose term," as ethicist Paul Ramsey notes, "for all forms of the complaint of the aggrieved moral nature against the harsh tenets of Calvinism.[10] Hence Edwards undertook *A Careful and Strict Enquiry into the Modern Prevailing Notions of that Freedom of Will, which is Supposed to be Essential to Moral Agency, Vertue and Vice, Reward and Punishment, Praise and Blame.* Here he accepts the postulate of modern science that everything is the effect of some prior cause, and reduces the Arminian position to absurdity by positing an infinite regress of freely willed actions behind each freely willed action. Each "free" act of the will must have been caused by something. On the one hand, if the only source of moral action is the "free" will, then each willing must have been "caused" by a previous willing—and so on. On the other hand, says Edwards, stating his own case, if even the will has to start somewhere, there must first be some motive or inclination toward action that the will then puts into effect. Human character and behavior then are rooted in the affections—in what William James calls the "center of personal energy." If the affections are pure, Edwards asserted, the actions of the will are good.

As Edwards observed, however, history, experience, and scripture show that human motives are notoriously impure. Christian theology has traditionally recognized this fact, as Edwards made plain in his massive treatise *The Great Christian Doctrine of Original Sin Defended; Evidences of it's Truth Produced, and Arguments to the Contrary Answered*. Edwards's doctrinal defense of original sin meshes with his philosophical analysis of the will, and both are in complete accord with his psychological investigation of the religious affections. Discounting the obvious surpluses of revivalistic enthusiasm, Edwards found that true religion consists of a divinely given new sense of the heart. Only with such a view of true religion does the nature of true virtue, the subject of Edwards's next work, become clear. For an individual with a new sense of the heart, it makes sense to say that true virtue "consists in *benevolence to being in general*. Or perhaps, to speak more accurately, it is that consent, propensity and union of heart to being in general, which is immediately exercised in a general good will."[11] In the virtue of such regenerate people, one sees the end for which God created the world—the subject of Edwards's final completed work—the emanation of God's own infinite fullness, the unbounded effulgence of the divine glory.

Edwards had envisioned his next project, "a History of the Work of Redemption, a body of divinity in an entire new method, being thrown into the form of a history,"[12] when he accepted a call in 1757 to become president of what is now Princeton University. Early in 1758 a reaction to a smallpox inoculation took his life. Because his thought ranged widely and was fertile, one finds a number of images of Edwards emerging in the interpretive introductions to the complete edition of his writings that is now being published. Certainly his articulation of the new sense of the heart provides ready access to the experiences of the Awakening. Other aspects of his thinking are also important, but his theological psychology gives the liveliest sense of the man in his own time. Early death leaves an aura of incompleteness over Edwards's life, yet his thought was sufficiently systematic to furnish some clear insights into the passions surrounding the Great Awakening.

No doubt there were excesses, indeed delusions, as Boston's Charles Chauncy and other "establishment" opponents charged. Unstable leaders like James Davenport led people into extravagances that were later regretted. Declared *non compos mentis* and expelled from Boston, and before that deported from Connecticut, in 1743 Davenport collected such "vanities" as the clothing of his female followers, for burning along with the books of "unconverted" ministers. Flames consumed the books on the wharf at New London, but someone spared the clothes. Davenport was the more colorful figure, but Edwards's theological psychology articulates the way spiritual deliverance was actually experienced by many colonial Americans. Whether sparked by the powerful oratory of the "Grand Itinerant," George Whitefield, or by the newly inspired preaching of their own clergy, many Americans were given a new sense of personal wholeness, granted by and anchored in the felt reality of God. This new sense of integrated and divinely accepted selfhood released the ambivalent tensions of declining Puritanism and liberated awakened believers in America's rapidly changing social and political circumstances. In William James's words, the kind of deliverance they experienced was precisely apposite to their previous uneasiness. For these newly awakened men and women, religion was once again a vital aspect of human life. From now on, the "twice-born" would set the pattern for spiritual experience in America.

Throughout the eighteenth-century Western world, "Pietism" was a significant countercurrent to the reigning assumptions and values of the Age of Reason. So the Great Awakening in America may be seen in connection with the efflorescence of "heart religion" in England and Europe. Whitefield himself saw it as a transatlantic phenomenon. Yet several important associations, implications, and consequences make it essential to view the Great Awakening as an episode in the history of religion in America.

First, Conrad Cherry is correct in stressing the need to see Edwards primarily as a theologian of faith in the tradition of John Calvin. But Perry Miller is also right in suggesting that Edwards's definition of God as "BEING IN GENERAL"—together with Edwards's own mystical sensitivity to God in nature—initiate an American way of thinking that culminates in the Transcendentalism of Ralph Waldo Emerson. Jonathan Edwards is in fact a transitional figure, who, in the complex integrity of his thinking, provides a passage between Puritan and later ways of being religious in America.

Second, the Great Awakening initiated revivalistic practices and evangelical priorities that have characterized American church life ever since. Churches geared toward conversions and missions began to dominate the American religious scene. These orientations did not become definitive until the Second Great Awakening of the early nineteenth century. But their roots certainly reach back to the revivals of Edwards's day.

Third, in addition to its experiential religiousness, the Awakening had revolutionary social and political implications. Perry Miller has pointed out the "democratizing" effects of revivalism: the laity began to speak out, and an awareness of their intercolonial ties began to grow among newly awakened believers. Alan Heimert has argued weightily that "New Light," pro-revival ministers fueled the fires of rebellion more assiduously than did the more "rational," restrained, and "enlightened" liberal clergy. These complex developments deserve more direct attention as we explore the role of religion in the next major episode in our history—the American Revolution.

NOTES

1. *Sydney E. Ahlstrom, ed., Theology in America: The Major Protestant Voices from Puritanism to Neo-Orthodoxy* (Indianapolis: The Bobbs-Merrill Company, Inc., 1967), pp. 33-37.

2. Richard L. Bushman, *From Puritan to Yankee: Character and the Social Order in Connecticut, 1690-1765* (Cambridge: Harvard University Press, 1967), p. 187.

3. William James, *The Varieties of Religious Experience* (New York: Macmillan Publishing Co., Inc., 1961), p. 393.

4. Ibid., pp. 393-94.

5. Ibid., p. 396.

6. Ibid., pp. 220-22.

7. Ibid., p. 387.

8. Quoted in Sydney E. Ahlstrom, *A Religious History of the American People* (New Haven: Yale University Press, 1972), p. 298.

9. Jonathan Edwards, *Religious Affections*, ed. by John E. Smith (New Haven: Yale University Press, 1959), p.1.

10. Jonathan Edwards, *Freedom of the Will*, ed. by Paul Ramsey (New Haven: Yale University Press, 1957), p. 3.

11. Jonathan Edwards, *The Nature of True Virtue* (Ann Arbor: The University of Michigan Press, 1960), p. 3.

12. Jonathan Edwards, from a letter of 19 October 1757 to the Trustees of the College of New Jersey at Princeton, included in Ahlstrom, *Theology*, p. 190.

3

THE POLITICAL FAITH OF '76: RELIGION AND POLITICS IN REVOLUTIONARY AMERICA

Historian Sydney E. Ahlstrom points out that

> in political terms, the four decades between the end of the "Old French War" and the election of Thomas Jefferson as president of the United States divide with a minimum of confusion into four fairly definite periods, each of them very familiar to most Americans:
>
> | | |
> |---|---|
> | 1760-1775 | A time of deteriorating relations with England and of growing sentiment for independence |
> | 1775-1783 | A time of war, reorganization, and state-forming |
> | 1783-1789 | The so-called Critical Period during which the problems of federalism were exposed, fiercely contended and officially resolved |
> | 1789-1800 | The Federalist Period in United States history, a period of crucial self-definition during which the problems of federal union under the Constitution and foreign relations of the new state were settled.[1] |

It all seems so clear! Yet on 5 July 1780, Abigail Adams, writing as "Portia" to "My Dearest Friend," said "who ever takes a retrospective view of the war in which we are engaged, will find that Providence has so intermixed our successes, and our defeats, that on the one hand we have not been left to despond, nor on the other, to be unduely elated."[2] How shall we make sense of the role of religion in a time when so much was changing so fast?

Americans often think of their nation—especially of its origins—in religious terms. We remember Pilgrims and Puritans "risking their all" for "religious freedom" in the New World. Historians use such religious metaphors as righteous empire and redeemer nation to describe the developing national consciousness. It is surprising, then, to learn that during the American Revolution church attendance was remarkably low. Such religious malaise seems even stranger because it came on the heels of the widespread revivals and heated theological controversies of the Great Awakening. Describing the revolutionary era as an Age of Politics, historian Edmund S. Morgan writes:

> In 1740 America's leading intellectuals were clergymen and thought about theology; in 1790 they were statesmen and thought about politics. A variety of forces, some of them reaching deep into the colonial past, helped to bring about the transformation, but it was so closely associated with the revolt from England that one may consider the American Revolution, as an intellectual movement, to mean the substitution of political for clerical leadership and of politics for religion as the most challenging area of human thought and endeavor.[3]

Hence church historians have probed the antecedents and consequences of the Revolution, but the religious dimensions of the Revolution itself—apart from the significant contributions of the "black regiment" of the clergy—have only recently been directly essayed.

As historian Mark A. Noll argues, the nature of religion in America before and after the Revolution does not become clear until we understand the role of religion in the Revolution. Indeed, the low ebb of church life during the War for Independence and the framing of the Constitution is anomalous until we pay attention to what a contemporary called "the principles and political faith of

'76.''⁴ When Americans turned from revivals to revolution, religion was not left behind. It simply changed shape. In fact, the revolutionary era cannot be fully understood until we think of politics as a possible form of religion.

Students of modernity have learned to speak of religion as "a means of ultimate transformation" and so to view many large-scale cultural changes as "religious.''⁵ But such liberating language sounds vague or abstract until it is tied to actual historical events. An examination of the relationship between religion and politics elucidates how "the political faith of '76" interacted with more traditional religion in the revolutionary period. In the midst of many conflicts, an important new form of religion was developing.

Just as there are many different kinds of political structures and many varieties of religion, so there is a wide range of possible relations between religion and politics. In a theocracy, a particular religion dominates politics. Under totalitarianism, the state often aggressively suppresses religious practices. In many modern societies, church and state are separated. One effect of the American Revolution was to alter significantly the pattern of relations between religion and politics and to broaden—through the federal Constitution—religious freedom in the United States.

Political ideology and action—in the case of a "holy war," for example, waged by a "divine" king—may itself be a form of religion. Clearly this usually is not the case. Indeed, the smooth functioning of a complex society may require an explicit differentiation between the religious and political realms of life. Yet, for a brief time during the American Revolution, political thought and activity were characterized by religious convictions. The short-lived conflation of religion and politics during the Revolution is important in two respects; first, it heightened the kinds of commitments the colonists made to the War for Independence; and, second, it set the scene for the emergence of forms of religion which were most characteristic of modern America. These were religious freedom, denominationalism, and the so-called civil religion.

To understand how politics can be a form of religion, we must remember that during the revolutionary period America was becoming, in Seymour Martin Lipset's fine phrase, "the first new nation." Hence political scientists' studies of recently developing nations could provide insights into the role of religion at the time of the American Revolution. Students of Third World nations often describe their sweeping social changes in terms of "cultural nationalism." We can see that something analogous was happening during the revolutionary epoch in America. For example, Donald E. Smith notes that modernization is fundamentally a process of differentiation, "by which integralist sacral societies governed by religio-political systems are being transformed into pluralist desacralized societies directed by greatly expanded secular polities."[6] During such transformations, politicians manipulate religion by using sacred symbols to organize disparate groups into movements for social change.

As an important source of attitudes and values, religion contributes to the underlying propensities and psychological dimensions of the political system—what Gabriel A. Almond and G. Bingham Powell, Jr., call "political culture."[7] Religion is not all doctrine and · spirituality; its symbols and values can energize and legitimate programs for political action. Nor are such close relations between religion and politics accidental. They grow from newly perceived characteristics of the society's religious traditions. Yet when the initial turbulence of political development passes, and a new nation emerges, we can expect to see—in the Third World or in the framing of the United States Constitution—politics again becoming secular and religion resuming a more churchly cast.

According to political theorist David E. Apter, "political religion" exists when "the state and the regime take on sacred characteristics," for then "the sacred characteristic becomes essential to maintaining solidarity in the community . . . [thus] giving sacrosanct qualities to the new state." So a political religion legitimates a particular regime, and the political regime is reinforced by "a renewed interest in a semimythical past, to produce antecedents for the regime" and often also by "a persistent attack upon a particular enemy." In these ways, "the 'birth' of the nation is thus a religious event," and "the agent of rebirth is normally an individual . . . who, as the leader of the political movement, is midwife to the birth of the nation."[8] John Adams remarked, for example, that George Washington was treated as a demigod. Apter's and Smith's ideas, however, have a wider usefulness.

When we think of the revolutionary period as a time of political development, it becomes clear that the character of American religion changed dramatically in a very short time. From the Stamp Act crisis through the War for Independence, American political religion was essentially what Apter calls a "mobilization system." That is, specific political goals were seen as transcendent ends, were often expressed in millennial terms, and were perceived as stages in the creation of a new kind of selfhood. But, with the Treaty of Paris, Americans confronted the problems of governing the new states and administering the confederacy. Hence the hopeful, energizing fervor of the war years passed, and American political religion changed into what Apter calls a "reconciliation system." With the framing of the federal Constitution came a preoccupation with law in terms of maintaining checks and balances of political power, a sense that individual dignity was bound together with the necessity of representative government, a commitment to the separation of church and state, and a recognition of the civil necessity of churchly religion.

Professor Apter regards mobilization systems as unstable in the long run. Reconciliation systems, he says, are by far the better kind of political religion for the orderly, ongoing life of modern society. Even though he does not discuss the American case, we can take a clue from Apter's work. Turning to the revolutionary period, we should look not only for the nature of American political religion, but also for the reasons why our Founding Fathers instituted a reconciliation rather than a mobilization system. Exploring the transition between these two kinds of political religions helps us to understand the political culture of the revolutionary period, and also to appreciate the appeal still generated in our own time by the political faith of '76.

The possibility that religion may affect the thought and action of a political culture recalls the earlier claim that religion is an aspect of human life. Even at its most spiritual, religion exists in and through human reality. Hence an acquaintance with the social life of eighteenth-century America is essential for understanding the role of religion in the revolutionary era. Throughout the early and middle eighteenth century, widespread social changes were under way—processes so far-reaching that historians have argued that "social change was in several ways a major energizer of the intricate [political] exchanges which ultimately and half-inadvertently gave us the Constitution."[9] Historian Kenneth A. Lockridge outlines several important changes that seemed to threaten the "comparatively isolated, static, homogeneous society" of the 1720s. The population of colonial America was becoming increasingly dense, outstripping its ability to open new settlements. Cultivable land became scarce in settled areas; sons either had to divide inherited farm lands or migrate. Because such divisions were limited by the requirements of subsistence, migration increased. Also because land was scarce, some men became wealthy while others became poor. Wealth was increasingly concentrated among the new "gentlemen," whose prosperity led to increasing polarization between themselves and the poor. The level and rate of social differentiation increased, as did the level of commercialization. Americans became more dependent upon their commercial relations, with each other and with world markets, for economic survival. Because the population and commerce grew simultaneously, there was little or no increase in aggregate per capita production or income.

These social changes meant that the expectations of young Americans also changed, and new possibilities together with new frustrations led to more contact between the people and the sources of political power. Individuals increased their demands upon the political system. Lockridge sees certain major political consequences of social change in prerevolutionary America. Political concerns arose about the corruption and "Europeanization" the concentration of wealth might bring to the increasingly polarized society. Virtually every social change challenged the isolation, independence, homogeneity, and continuity of rural America, posing "a threat not simply to its economic interests but perhaps to an integral world view." In addition, "when one considers that religion usually pervades the rural world view, it is easy to imagine that many Americans of the eighteenth century could have become convinced that their world was coming to an end by action of the devil himself."[10] Earlier life was increasingly idealized, and continuing changes seemed more threatening; a "psychologically snowballing" effect was at work. Hence "much of rural America was made ripe for a very special kind of political mobilization by the social changes of the eighteenth century."[11]

Lockridge finds other results as well. He notes that "the Revolution completed this mobilization by offering a crusading ideology under which this segment of society could undertake political action, which otherwise their own world view condemned." Yet "out of the total experience of diversity and of political mobilization there emerged ever more men with an acceptance of the clash of interests and beliefs, men who literally found themselves in the choices they had to or wanted to make. These 'modernized' men were still few, but as they were too many to be merely the leaders and mediators of society, they formed a constituency."[12] Finally, increasing demands undercut the credibility of the old colonial elite. Heightened conflicts gave them more opportunities to fail as mediators; the old elite was in a precarious position—symbolized in the ordeal of Thomas Hutchinson—on the eve of the Revolution.

The changes Lockridge outlines created a situation in which certain political ideas moved people with religious force. Articulated often in response to events perceived as encroachments upon American life, these political ideas were crucial. In the decade before Independence, many colonists idealized the previous century and a half of American experience. "This intimate relationship between Revolutionary thought and the circumstances of life in eighteenth-century America," as historian Bernard Bailyn notes, "endowed the Revolution with its peculiar force and made it so profoundly a transforming event."[13]

To understand the remarkable coalescence of social change, political thought, economic development, and religious convictions in the revolutionary era, one should examine several important symbols which united these otherwise diverse aspects of American life. Such symbols were polyvalent, and their capacity of uniting perceptions and values from several aspects of life made them broadly and deeply appealing. Even beyond their individual attraction, these symbols meshed to form a pattern of meaning powerful enough to motivate a revolution and lead men to form a new nation. The needs of a victoriously independent people brought a realignment of their central symbols distinguishing the spirit of the federal Constitution from the political faith of '76. But, for a crucial period, the pattern formed by these polyvalent symbols empowered the political religion of the American Revolution.

The American Revolution, as historian Gordon S. Wood has shown, "was actually many revolutions at once, the product of a complicated culmination of many diverse personal grievances and social strains" directed against "the remotely rooted and awkwardly imposed imperial system" of Britain.[14] There was great disagreement over ideas among the revolutionaries, and considerable dissatisfaction at the lower levels of society with the revolutionary leadership. And there were many sincere loyalists. Yet for a brief period the imperial crisis united America geographically and ideologically as never before. The spirit just before and during the first years of the fighting was strong enough, even as its fervor faded, to animate Americans and to sustain their War for Independence. But the unity, however powerful, was over almost before it started.

A rush of unforeseen events soon required Americans to find new ways of coping with changing political problems, and, as Wood observes, "in the process old ideas, old images were twisted and eventually shattered."[15] Fortunately, there was a federal solution for the breakdown of the revolutionary synthesis. The central symbols shifted their meanings and associations; a large-scale alteration of the revolutionary pattern preserved its achievements; the new nation had not only a beginning, but a future. What were the symbols that moved men to war and, realigned, created the American republic? Were they political, social, economic, or religious or a combination?

The principal cultural symbols of revolutionary America fall into two groups: those with positive, hopeful associations and those with negative, discouraging implications. Perhaps the negative symbols are easier to understand. Two dark symbols recur in the rhetoric of the period—tyranny and corruption. The colonists saw both economic and political tyranny in the actions of Parliament between the French and Indian War and the Declaration of Independence. In addition to the Quebec Act and the Proclamation of 1763, Americans perceived taxes, duties, quotas—along with the personnel to enforce and collect them—as attempts to regulate and derive unmerited British profit from the growing commerce of the colonies. And for such attempts to be made by a legislative body in which Americans had no real voice looked like political oppression as well. When rumors of the appointment of Anglican bishops to the colonies began to circulate, British tyranny seemed unbounded. In Jefferson's words, a pattern appeared to emerge, "a deliberate, systematical plan of reducing us to slavery."[16] Americans like John Adams took it all personally, blaming the English Crown for an "execrable Project . . . set on foot for my Ruin as well as that of America in General."[17]

Closely linked to tyranny was the widespread use of the symbol of corruption. Alternately fascinated and repulsed by the luxury they observed abroad, Americans saw the fruit of economic success in pejorative moral terms and called it corruption. London looked especially degenerate. England, Americans felt, "once the land of liberty—the school of patriots—the nurse of heroes, has become the land of slavery—the school of parricides and the nurse of tyrants."[18] The present English moral and economic sickness was linked to political corruption; even the revered English law had been tainted beyond repair. But the American desire to repristinate the English legal system in the New World was made ambivalent by another, increasingly apparent source of corruption—within themselves. "Alas! Great Britain," wrote a Virginian in 1775, "their vices have even extended to America."[19] On 13 February 1779, "Portia" Adams asked her "Dearest Friend":

> And does my Friend think that there are no hopes of peace? Must we still endure the Desolations of war with all the direfull consequences attending it. —I fear we must and that America is less and less worthy of the blessings of peace.
>   Luxery that bainfull poison has unstrung and enfeabled her sons. The soft penetrating plague has insinuated itself into the freeborn mind, blasting that noble ardor, that impatient Scorn of base subjection which formerly distinguished your Native Land, and the Benevolent wish of general good will is swallowed up by a Narrow selfish Spirit, by a spirit of oppression and extortion.[20]

The corruption they saw in themselves showed Americans the necessity of some great transformation and pushed them anxiously toward a break with Britain and to revolution, before it was too late.

If the social frustrations of eighteenth-century America were the result of declining virtue, the Calvinists were not surprised. Not all the colonists shared their theology, but many agreed that something had to be done—once and for all—to save the colonies from British degeneracy and from the corruption spreading through America. The internal conversion experiences of the Great Awakening were not forgotten. Days of "humiliation" and prayers linked the colonies together in confessions of sin—rites of purification on the eve of Revolution.

There was also a cluster of positive cultural symbols offsetting the specter of tyranny and corruption. In 1792 in his *Advice to the Privileged Orders in the Several States of Europe,* Joel Barlow argued that certain beliefs or "habits of thinking" had been the source of the American Revolution—principally the belief *"that all men are equal in their rights."*[21] Political, economic, and religious, "equality represented the social source from which the anticipated harmony and public virtue of the New World would flow," in the words of Gordon S. Wood, who concludes appropriately that "it was a beautiful but ambiguous ideal."[22] Were Americans committed to equality of opportunity, or to a fully egalitarian concept of their condition? This ambiguity generated debate and, together with the convictions of spiritual equality spread by the revivals of the Awakening, made equality an unstable but positive symbol of the times.

Allied closely with equality, yet suffering none of its ambivalence, was the symbol of liberty. The spirit of freedom from economic, political, and religious tyranny seemed to be fleeing the Old World and, as William Hooper wrote in 1776, "seeking an asylum westward."[23] On 20 April 1771, Abigail Adams wrote to Isaac Smith, Jr., expressing the connection between these two symbols:

> Are not the people here more upon an Eaquality in point of knowledg and of circumstances—there being none so immensely rich as to Lord it over us, neither any so abjectly poor as to suffer for the necessaries of life provided they will use the means. It has heretofore been our boasted priviledg that we could sit under our own vine and Apple trees in peace enjoying the fruits of *our own labor*—but alass! the much dreaded change Heaven avert. Shall we ever wish to

change Countries; to change conditions with the Affricans and the Laplanders for sure it were better never to have known the blessings of Liberty than to have enjoyed it, and then to have it ravished from us.[24]

Responsible personal freedom was possible only where there was public or civil liberty. In America this required a revolution. It was as clear as that.

The patriots were convinced that true liberty depended upon the sacrifice of private interests to the public good. Curious blend of Puritans and utopians that they were, colonial spokesmen believed that their compatriots would make these sacrifices and that public life would become pure and harmonious. Like the Puritans, the revolutionaries wanted freedom to control things as they saw fit and, as they sometimes admitted, for their own profit. The notion of civil virtue was a powerful symbol. So strong a concern with public moral quality could be satisfied only in a republic, whose creation required a revolution.

Together with the patriots' commitment to public virtue was an abiding interest in the present and future character of the New World's inhabitants. Hence "the people" became another resounding cultural symbol. All men and institutions placed above the people were widely mistrusted. Removal of such hindrances and oppressions would allow the people to manifest their natural goodness. Such ardent Americans as Tom Paine were so anxious to create a pure public identity that, forgetting the private side of their Puritan heritage, they did not foresee that an excess of power in the people could lead to a new kind of tyranny. Yet many leaders of the resistance worried about the people's potential abuse of the power they could gain in the revolution. For them, as George Washington noted later, "We have, probably, had too good an opinion of human nature in forming our confederation."[25] The attainment of public liberty might reveal new complexities in the moral quality of the people, but, before and during the War for Independence, these symbols came together naturally.

If any symbol dominated the consciousness of revolutionary America, it was republicanism. All the other symbols—positive and negative—were involved in this powerful idea. The colonists' commitment to republicanism—a new order of relations for a renewed people—meant that the War for Independence was more than a local rebellion against an oppressive English system. As Gordon Wood wrote, "it was meant to be a social revolution of the most profound sort."[26] Beyond their positive convictions, even American doubts about themselves fed their desires for republicanism. In wanting to found their own republic, Americans were rejecting not only England and Europe but the whole world as they understood it—and themselves—to have been. Only a profound "faith in the regenerative effects of republican government itself on the character of the people," says Wood, "can explain the idealistic fervor of the Revolutionary leaders in 1776."[27]

If many individuals had experienced inward spiritual conversions during the Great Awakening, American society as a whole now seemed ready for rebirth. The colonists wanted to be reborn as their fathers had been. In the words of Benjamin Rush, the mainspring of their commitment lay in their belief that "the Revolution w .ı all its evocation of patriotism and the martial spirit would cleanse the American soul of its impurities" and, Rush hoped, introduce "among us the same temperance in pleasure, the same modesty in dress, the same justice in business, and the same veneration for the name of the Deity which distinguished our ancestors."[28]

These several powerful cultural symbols were ultimately legitimated, and the actions they called for were sanctioned, by a unique and finally unstable compound of radical Whig politics, Enlightenment rationalism, and Reformed theology. Because, as Gordon Wood notes, "for the republican patriots of 1776 the commonweal was all-encompassing—a transcendent object with a unique moral worth that made partial considerations fade into insignificance,"[29] it is fair to speak of the political faith of '76 as a political religion and, specifically in David Apter's terms, as a mobilization system. Professors Bailyn and Wood have argued persuasively that radical Whig republicanism gave the American Revolution its political ideology. The Whig desire to remake English politics by resurrecting the quasi-mythical purity of Anglo-Saxon law appears to have made republicanism especially open to certain religious convictions. What contributions from the Enlightenment and from Reformed Protestantism gave the Revolution its religious resources and power? Why did this combination, which inspired and sustained a Revolution, so soon fall apart?

Part of the explanation lies in the events of the times; part lies in the nature of the ideas themselves. The political leaders of the American Revolution found Enlightenment ideas and rhetoric naturally suited to their needs. Peter Gay has described one major thrust of the Enlightenment in terms of criticism. Enlightened thinkers challenged standing assumptions in all areas of life. So their thinking seemed ready-made for people who wanted to achieve political independence from the "tyranny" and "corruption" of the British Imperial system. The Enlightenment belief that social and political relations should be founded on the principles of reason and nature—what Thomas Jefferson called "the common sense of the matter"—meshed with the radical Whig attempt to reform present British corruptions and to reestablish the purity and harmony of Anglo-Saxon law. By anchoring social and political criticism in the universal nature of reason, Enlightenment thought sanctioned the active political criticism which fed the Revolution.

Any attempt to trace the sources of the American Enlightenment leads to the observation that there were several varieties of the Enlightenment in Europe, helping to explain how Americans could be selective in their adoption of Enlightened principles and beliefs. Henry F. May has demonstrated that American revolutionary leaders assimilated a moderate English Enlightenment—the political thought of Locke and the radical Whigs. And the pragmatic, empirical epistemology of Scottish "common sense" realism provided philosophical support for American practical approaches to experience in general. The radical skepticism of David Hume and the French philosophes had little impact in America, however, and the revolutionary Enlightenment associated with political turbulence in France attracted Americans only briefly.[30]

Enlightenment thinking was powerful in the revolutionary period in America because it provided a way of uniting religious commitment and public responsibility. It was a way to anchor what Donald H. Meyer calls the central theme of the American Enlightenment, namely the belief that "faith and reason, in harmony, would serve the national interest."[31] Enlightened thought, as Americans assimilated it, was not a matter of abstract rationality.

Rather, it was a way of relating universal, transcendent principles of reason—and secular analogues, such as Benjamin Franklin's belief in an all-consuming Providence—to practical social, political, and moral concerns. As such, Enlightenment ideas provided ultimate sanctions for the cultural symbols that moved Americans of many persuasions to unite in revolution. The Enlightenment was culturally powerful in America for a brief time because it supplied a rhetoric of ultimacy for polyvalent symbols. By linking their social, economic, and political desires to the universal nature of reason, Enlightenment principles gave Americans a "cosmic" background for revolution. The crucial congruence between Enlightenment truths and the colonists' religious traditions enabled a political religion to develop and mobilize Americans toward a successful revolution.

Americans of disparate ranks and backgrounds shared the frustrations of widespread social change and a common political goal. Because people never fit neatly into the historian's categories of "faith and reason," the American Enlightment was, in the words of Joseph Ellis:

> less a period of protracted warfare between the advocates of faith and the advocates of reason than a time when American intellectuals blended or balanced opposing elements. Perhaps words like "virtue" or "moral," or even a term like "natural law," became so popular because they allowed a writer to refer simultaneously to both spiritual and rational realms, to fuse opposites in a language that all Americans found meaningful and enlightening.[32]

Enlightenment thought and criticism provided the philosophical linkage between politics and religion in America.

The Protestant Reformed tradition, the spiritual heritage of so many American colonists, joined the Enlightenment in the political religion of the Revolution. It too possessed a tradition of criticism, and it too interpreted human experience in ways that further empowered the cultural symbols of the time. Scholars such as Perry Miller have shown how many Protestant clergymen espoused the revolutionary cause and sometimes even led their people into battle. Alan Heimert has presented evidence that the revival-oriented, New Light Calvinist clergy were more ardent revolutionaries than the rational and respectable ministers of long-established churches in commercial centers. Or perhaps more accurately, as Nathan Hatch argues, both Old and New Light ministers joined in "a political religion of *the* New England clergy," the antecedents of which lie more directly in the Anglo-French wars than in vestiges of the Great Awakening.[33] Despite the diversity that Mark A. Noll finds among American Christians in the revolutionary era, the rhetoric of the clergy was powerful, and the sacrifices of the soldiers were extensive, because the values of Reformed Protestantism united with radical Whig politics and Enlightenment truths, creating a public realm where revolution was perceived as a means of ultimate transformation.

Reformed Protestantism was critical of established ideas and institutions. The Puritan struggle to reform the Church of England was a remembered precursor to the later colonists' desire to redress the corruptions of the British Imperial system and reinstitute the purity of life under Anglo-Saxon law. The influence of Puritan thought had made Americans sensitive to tyranny and enemies of corruption, particularly in the sense of "degenerate" institutions and "spiritual snares" and "temptations." With its strong sense of sinful corruption, Puritanism prepared Americans to inculcate virtue in the people and strive for purity in the public realm.

Well before the political revolution, Americans believed in the necessity of regeneration and yearned for the spiritual liberty of reborn men. Their religious thinking was similarly geared to the dawn of a new age, a millennium of order and peace following heightened spiritual conflict and a bloody war. In addition to Protestant doctrines of human finitude and the need for fundamental law, Edmund S. Morgan ties the central Reformed idea of the "calling" to the political and economic convictions of the Revolutionary period:

> The Puritan Ethic whether enjoined by God, by history, or by philosophy, called for diligence in a productive calling, beneficial to both society and to the individual. It encouraged frugality and frowned on extravagance. It viewed the merchant with suspicion and speculation with horror. It distrusted prosperity and gathered strength from adversity. It prevailed widely among Americans of different times and places, but those who urged it most vigorously always believed it to be on the point of expiring and in need of renewal.

> The role of these ideas in the American Revolution—during the period, say, roughly from 1764 to 1789—was not explicitly causative. . . . Yet the major developments, the resistance to Great Britain, independence, the divisions among the successful Revolutionists, and the formulation of policies for the new nation, were all discussed and understood by men of the time in terms derived from the Puritan Ethic. And the way men understood and defined issues before them frequently influenced their decisions.[34]

Considering how these elements of the Reformed tradition merged with political, economic, and social concerns into the reigning symbols mobilizing Americans during the revolutionary era, we can agree with Morgan's conclusion that "Patriotism and Puritanism marched hand in hand from 1764-1789."[35] Given the symbolic coinherence of Reformed Protestantism, Enlightenment reason and virtue, and radical Whig political ideology, it is not surprising that the American Revolution looks like a collective conversion experience—a religious regeneration in the form of politics.

Seeing the revolutionary era in this way illumines the cultural changes that occurred when the cohesion of these influences began to dissolve. After fighting and winning a War for Independence from the tyranny and corruption of the British Imperial system, Americans were confronted by a new set of problems. If the Revolution relied on principles of criticism, the task of building their own system of government required new ideas. Symbols and values that had sustained protest and rebellion before were not needed. Indeed, several of the very symbols sanctioning the Revolution created new problems. Gordon S. Wood has shown in great detail how men of power came to believe that the people were now exercising their own kind of tyranny. Trials of state governments and constitutions changed many minds and made the federal scheme of a national Constitution seem necessary, even attractive.[36]

When it became apparent that the Revolution had not opened a new age of virtuous equality, political leaders began to see the need for "checks and balances" within a representative government. "Power naturally grows," said John Adams, "because human passions are insatiable. But that power alone can grow which already is too great; that which is unchecked; that which has no equal power to control it."[37] Tom Paine no longer was a hero. The Federalists proposed a constitution that did not rely on public virtue. In Federalist Paper Number Ten, James Madison argued for the beneficial value of the permanency of factions within a nation. The people ratified the Constitution and formed a government acknowledging differences of interest and providing ways of coping with ongoing conflicts between various constituencies of the new nation. In the next decade, the bloody excesses of the French Revolution turned many Americans away from imported Enlightenments; reliance on reason alone became associated with political terror.

If the Revolution did not improve the public moral quality of the people, neither did its constellation of symbols meet their need for inward spiritual experience. The new government instituted religious freedom, but it took a long time for all the states to disavow established religions. New revivals began in the 1790s, and the beginning of the nineteenth century saw widespread religious enthusiasm—some said a Second Great Awakening. Church patterns and practices (now called denominationalism) developed, defining church life for subsequent generations. The Founding Fathers were men of the Enlightenment, but the early years of Jefferson's presidency coincided with a powerful reemergence of ecclesiastical Protestantism. If God had blessed the Revolution as a "Moral Governor," he soon came back as Jehovah. The Age of Reason gave way to what H. Richard Niebuhr calls "the Kingdom of Christ."[38]

The next chapter investigates the religious and social implications of the rebirth of Protestantism following the revolutionary era. But first we should look at an additional consequence of the shift from the mobilization system of the political faith of '76 to the reconciliation system of 1787. The political religion of the Revolution ushered in American church life as we know it, but denominationalism was not always sufficient for the spiritual needs of later Americans. In our day, some seek to resurrect the political faith of '76—or "civil religion." Our study of the revolutionary era should enable us to interpret this attractive nostalgia.

The public realm of revolutionary America is often pictured as united toward goals of liberty, equality, and self-determination.

The myth is far from fallacious. Indeed, we have seen how a cohesive set of polyvalent cultural symbols unified frustrations and hopes, and mobilized Americans for a successful revolution. But there were many reluctant patriots—and many Tories—on the scene during the Revolution, and discord was not uncommon. To understand the dissension of the time, we must recognize that religions— whether expressed in political or other cultural forms—often get their start in times of uncertainty. Later generations tend to enshrine their interpretation of a religion's beginnings to help meet the challenges of new situations. Hence we would expect Americans in later times of stress to recall—perhaps even to make extravagant claims for—the political faith of '76.

As Stephen B. Oates observes, for example, Abraham Lincoln asked Americans of his day to:

> "swear by the blood of the Revolution" to respect and obey the laws and stop all violence and killing. Let reverence for the law be sung by every mother to her child, "let it be preached from the pulpit, proclaimed in legislative halls, and enforced in courts of justice. And, in short, let it become the *political religion* of the nation; and let the old and the young, the rich and the poor, the grave and the gay, of all sexes and tongues, and colors and conditions, sacrifice unceasingly upon its altars."[39]

In our time, sociologist Robert N. Bellah has become an advocate for what, following Rousseau, he calls "civil religion," contending that:

> While some have argued that Christianity is the national faith, and others that church and synagogue celebrate only the generalized religion of "the American Way of Life," few have realized that there actually exists alongside of and rather clearly differentiated from the churches an elaborate and well-institutionalized civil religion in America. . . . Not only . . . [is] there . . . such a thing, but also . . . this religion—or perhaps better, this religious dimension—has its own seriousness and integrity and requires the same care in understanding that any other religion does.[40]

Yet even when patriotic rhetoric is underscored by periodic references to the divine in presidential inaugural addresses, such "civil religion" will not suffice for contemporary Americans.

Whatever the term "modernization" means—industrialization, bureaucratization, urbanization (the definitions are legion)—it is clear that at least one aspect of modernity involves increasing differentiation between structures of consciousness (such as religion and politics) and increasing individualization within them. Politics is less closely tied to religion in complex societies, as Bellah elsewhere contends, and spiritual experience tends to become a more private affair.[41] Now people find themselves pulled toward being political *and* religious—and many other things, too. The hard requirements of what T. S. Eliot aptly called "the dissociation of sensibility" are not well served by attempts to fuse religion and politics in the rhetoric of civil religion. Contemporary Americans may need new ways of being religious, but attempts to revive the political religion of the revolutionary era (as seen in President John Kennedy's appealing inaugural rhetoric) are now primarily nostalgic. Proponents of civil religion remind us that church traditions do not exhaust the roles of religion in American culture. But we cannot expect the political faith of '76 to supply a way of being religious that is adequate for the problems we now face.

Even in the late 1780s, when the Federalists employed populist rhetoric to advertise their relatively elitist scheme of government, the language of American civil virtue was becoming "merely" political. With the ratification of the Constitution, the cultural symbols of the Revolution shifted their meanings, and the various aspects of life once held together and mobilized by these symbols began to differentiate. Observing his countrymen's efforts to form a government, John Adams recognized there is "no special providence for Americans, and their nature is the same with that of others."[42] Although often forgotten, the lesson that Americans are not an exceptional people was learned early and institutionalized in 1787. Americans were historically fortunate insofar as social changes and a successful revolution led to a political framework that eased, and survived, the eventual modernization of American life.

Politics and religion often have been closely associated in American history, but never again with the transcendent legitimation given by the unique combination of radical Whig ideology, Enlightenment universal truths, and Reformed Protestantism to the political faith of '76. That faith helped to mobilize a changing society in a successful revolution. As the conflict that enabled the founding of our country, the Revolution has a lasting and inspiring place in our national consciousness. In some significant ways a religious event, the Revolution gave Americans political identity. But the continuing story of religion in America leads in different directions. While depending in important ways upon the political faith of '76, later generations discovered new ways of being religious in America.

NOTES

1. Sydney E. Ahlstrom, *A Religious History of the American People* (New Haven: Yale University Press, 1972), pp. 360-61.

2. L. H. Butterfield, Marc Friedlaender, and Mary-Jo Kline, eds., *The Book of Abigail and John: Selected Letters of the Adams Family, 1762-1784* (Cambridge, Mass.: Harvard University Press, 1975), p. 262.

3. Edmund S. Morgan, "The Revolutionary Era as an Age of Politics," in John R. Howe, Jr., ed., *The Role of Ideology in the American Revolution* (New York: Holt, Rinehart and Winston, 1970), p. 10.

4. Thomas Tredwell of New York, as quoted in Gordon S. Wood, *The Creation of the American Republic, 1776-1787* (New York: W. W. Norton and Company, Inc., 1972), p. 523.

5. For example, see Frederick J. Streng, Charles L. Lloyd, Jr., and Jay T. Allen, *Ways of Being Religious: Readings for a New Approach to Religion* (Englewood Cliffs, N. J.: Prentice-Hall, Inc., 1973), pp. 1-22.

6. Donald Eugene Smith, *Religion and Political Development* (Boston: Little, Brown and Company, 1970), p. 1.

7. Gabriel A. Almond and G. Bingham Powell, Jr., *Comparative Politics: A Developmental Approach* (Boston: Little, Brown and Co., 1966), p. 23.

8. David E. Apter, "Political Religion in the New Nations," in Clifford Geertz, ed., *Old Societies and New States: The Quest for Modernity in Asia and Africa* (New York: The Free Press of Glencoe, 1963), pp. 82-83.

9. Kenneth A. Lockridge, "Social Change and the Meaning of the American Revolution," *Journal of Social History* 6, no. 4 (Summer 1973): 405.

10. Ibid., p. 423.

11. Ibid., pp. 423-24.

12. Ibid., p. 428.

13. Bernard Bailyn, *The Ideological Origins of the American Revolution* (Cambridge, Mass.: The Belknap Press of Harvard University Press, 1976), pp. vi-vii.

14. Wood, *Creation of the American Republic*, p. 75.

15. Ibid., p. 282.

16. Thomas Jefferson, quoted in Wood, *Creation of the American Republic*, p. 39.

17. John Adams, quoted in Wood, *Creation of the American Republic*, p. 82 n.85.

18. Ibid., p. 32.

19. Ibid., p. 110.

20. Adams, quoted in Butterfield, *Book of Abigail and John*, p. 236.

21. Barlow, quoted in Wood, *Creation of the American Republic*, p. vii.

22. Wood, *Creation of the American Republic*, p. 73.

23. Hooper, quoted in Ibid., p. 43.

24. Adams, quoted in Butterfield, *Book of Abigail and John*, p. 50.

25. Washington, quoted in Wood, *Creation of the American Republic*, p. 472.

26. Wood, *Creation of the American Republic*, p. 91.

27. Ibid., pp. 120-21.

28. Rush, quoted in Ibid., p. 124.

29. Wood, *Creation of the American Republic*, p. 61.

30. Henry F. May, *The Enlightenment in America* (New York: Oxford University Press, 1976).

31. D. H. Meyer, "The Uniqueness of the American Enlightenment," *American Quarterly* 28, no. 2 (Summer 1976): 166.

32. Joseph Ellis, "Habits of Mind and an American Enlightenment," *American Quarterly* 28, no. 2 (Summer 1976): 158-59.

33. Perry Miller, "From the Covenant to the Revival," in James Ward Smith and A. Leland Jamison, eds., *The Shaping of American Religion* (Princeton: Princeton University Press, 1961), pp. 322-68; Alan Heimert, *Religion and the American Mind: From the Great Awakening to the Revolution* (Cambridge, Mass.: Harvard University Press, 1966); Nathan O. Hatch, *The Sacred Cause of Liberty: Republican Thought and the Millennium in Revolutionary New England* (New Haven: Yale University Press, 1977), p. 8.

34. Edmund S. Morgan, "The Puritan Ethic and the American Revolution," *The William and Mary Quarterly*, Third Series, 24, no. 4 (October 1967): 7-8.

35. Ibid., p. 42.

36. Wood, Parts Three, Four, Five, and Six.

37. Adams, quoted in Richard Hofstadter, *The American Political Tradition and the Men Who Made It* (New York: Alfred A. Knopf, 1964), p. 3.

38. Contra Catharine Albanese, *Sons of the Fathers* (Philadelphia: Temple University Press, 1976); H. Richard Niebuhr, *The Kingdom of God in America* (New York: Harper and Row, 1937), pp. 88-126.

39. Stephen B. Oates, *With Malice Toward None: The Life of Abraham Lincoln* (New York: Harper and Row, 1977), p. 47.

40. Robert N. Bellah, "Civil Religion in America." *Daedalus* 96, no. 1 (Winter 1967): 1; also see his "The Revolution and Civil Religion," in Jerald C. Brauer, ed., *Religion and the American Revolution* (Philadelphia: Fortress Press, 1976), pp. 55-73.

41. See Robert N. Bellah, "Religious Evolution," in William A. Lessa and Evon Z. Vogt, *Reader in Comparative Religion: An Anthropological Approach* (New York: Harper and Row, 1965), pp. 73-87; and his "Meaning and Modernisation," *Religious Studies* 4 (1968): 37-45.

42. Adams, quoted in Wood, *Creation of the American Republic*, p. 571.

4

RELIGIOUS FREEDOM, REVIVALISM, AND THE CHURCHES: A SOCIOLOGICAL APPROACH TO THE SECOND GREAT AWAKENING

Breaking from the previous history of the West, the Constitution of the United States established religious freedom as the law of the land. The "first new nation" would recognize no Church. The reasons for this novel development were many and complex. In terms of the events of the times, religious freedom introduced a new wave of revivalism. The colorful events from the "burned-over district" of New York State and the spiritual agitations on the Western frontier have led many historians to see revivalism as the distinguishing mark of a "Second Great Awakening." As Barton Stone described the results of a huge camp meeting he convened at Cane Ridge, Kentucky, in early August of 1801: "many things transpired there, which were so much like miracles, that if they were not, they had the same effects as miracles on infidels and unbelievers; for many of them by these were convinced that Jesus was the Christ, and bowed in submission to Him."[1]

Between ten thousand and twenty-five thousand otherwise isolated people spent a week together in the wilderness on this occasion. Historian Sydney E. Ahlstrom portrayed the scene:

> One must try first to re-create the scene: the milling crowds of hard-ened farmers, tobacco-chewing, tough-spoken, notoriously profane,

famous for their alcoholic thirst; their scarcely demure wives and large broods of children; the rough clearing, the rows of wagons and crude improvised tents with horses staked out behind; the gesticulating speaker on a rude platform, or perhaps simply a preacher holding forth from a fallen tree. At night, when the forest's edge was limned by the flickering light of many campfires, the effect of apparent miracles would be heightened. For men and women accustomed to retiring and rising with the birds, these turbulent nights must have been especially awe-inspiring. And underlying every other conditioning circumstance was the immense loneliness of the frontier farmer's normal life and the exhilaration of participating in so large a social occasion.[2]

The events were indeed colorful. As Barton Stone remembered in his autobiography:

The bodily agitations or exercises, attending the excitement in the beginning of this century, were various, and called by various names. . . . The falling exercise was very common among all classes, the saints and sinners of every age and every grade, from the philosopher to the clown. The subject of the exercise would, generally, with a piercing scream, fall like a log on the floor, earth, or mud, and appear as dead. . . .

The jerks cannot be so easily described. . . .

The dancing exercise . . . generally began with the jerks, and was peculiar to the professors of religion. . . .[3]

Stone also describes the barking, laughing, running, and singing exercises.

However brightly they blaze, revivals do not flare up on their own; nor do they burn unattended or brighten the sky forever. America had seen revivals before. What is most significant about both religious freedom and the revivals is the kind of social structures they transformed. In an atmosphere of religious freedom, American churches became organizations peculiarly able to fuel the revivals and, even more importantly, to sustain and direct their enormous energies even when the camp fires began to dim. Denominationalism seems so natural today we may forget what a radically new form of social organization it was in the early nineteenth century. A sociological approach can help us understand the emergence of denominationalism during the Second Great Awakening.

While its soul is often an intensely personal experience, religion is almost never a sheerly internal affair. An individual's spiritual experience yields a new sense of selfhood. That new spiritual identity reveals new ways of being involved with other people, new relations with those recognized as spiritual kin and with society at large. Joachim Wach concludes his *Sociology of Religion* by observing that "man, in his religious attitudes, seems to have, all through his history, at once felt very near and very far from his fellow man."[4] Since these mixed feelings of isolation and togetherness cause both the formation and the destruction of religious groups, the tensions they generate are vital forces in religious life. A profound personal experience, such as rebirth or conversion, brings in new social relations. Associations are formed with people whose spiritual experiences are similar to one's own. Missionary activities are undertaken to "spread the word," and so to bring others "into the fold."

A full understanding of religion thus requires an investigation of the special nature of religious groups and an exploration of how such groups interact with other forces in a given society. Max Weber, the founder of the sociology of religion, did not focus upon religion as such, but—as Talcott Parsons emphasizes—"upon *the relations between* religious ideas and commitments and other aspects of human conduct, especially the economic characteristics of human conduct within a society."[5] Such relations show how the social aspects of religion change over time.

Throughout human history, religion has become increasingly distinct from other aspects of life. Although we cannot fully understand their lives and artifacts, earlier peoples usually lived in more unified worlds of experience than we do. Like the American Puritans, their cultures were more cohesive or symbolically concentric than ours; religion integrated all of life by serving as its center. The diffusion of symbols in Puritanism needs to be seen in tandem with what sociologists call increasing institutional differentiation and social stratification. As societies become more complex, religion becomes a special aspect of life, with its own institutions, leaders, and theories, rather than remaining the symbolic center of a holistic world. Charting such broad changes is an enormously intriguing but essentially speculative task. As a hypothesis, however, the differentiation of religion from other aspects of social life illumines

America's Second Awakening. We will notice how, in a changing society, widespread and intensely personal spiritual experiences spurred the formation of distinctive religious institutions—the denominations—which, in turn, preserved and nurtured another way of being religious in America.

Now denominationalism is the official model of American church life. Well-established and strong, it is often used to describe the natural course of events. The entire history of religion in America has sometimes been written as the story of "mainline" denominations. But what we know as denominationalism could have begun only in the unique social and political climate of the early nineteenth century. The distinctive religious institutions which developed then must be seen in relation to the political and social strains of those times. Such a perspective will suggest why such powerful religious institutions may no longer fully suffice for contemporary Americans.

Although it soon came apart, the political faith of '76—that unique conflation of Enlightenment reason, radical Whig political ideology, and Reformed Protestantism—lasted long enough to sustain the Revolution and to provide a legal basis for the separation of church and state in America. Article VI of the Constitution stipulates that "no religious test shall ever be required as a qualification to any office or public trust under the United States," and the First Amendment provides that "Congress shall make no law respecting an establishment of religion, or prohibiting the free exercise thereof; or abridging the freedom of speech or of the press; or the right of the people peaceably to assemble and to petition the Government for a redress of grievances." Most of the individual states—as almost every previous sovereign polity in the history of Western Christendom—had an established church, but no single church organization had sufficient hegemony to become *the* Church of the new nation. Everywhere there was a measure of toleration or "connivance" at religious freedom, and each church body tended to recognize that its own continued existence depended upon its granting to others an equal right. While enlightened documents like James Madison's "Memorial and Remonstrance on the Religious Rights of Man" in 1784, and Thomas Jefferson's "Bill for Establishing Religious Freedom in Virginia" in 1796, provided a theoretical justification for this daring experiment, religious freedom actually came about because it was a practical necessity. Henceforth religious authority in America depended upon persuasion rather than coercion.

Together with religious freedom went the profound influence of the frontier in establishing basic social and cultural conditions. A line between civilization and the wilderness, the frontier was always moving west. Geographical movement was the mode of growth for the new nation; dislocation was social and cultural as well as physical. The tremendous energies of exploration and settlement reverberated to the more established East. The impact of the frontier was felt everywhere. The established churches of British colonies were not ideally suited to organize the religious experience of pioneers and westward settlers.

Life on the frontier was too hard, the work of settlement too draining, for its people to find solace in the civilized truths of enlightenment thought. Its rude exhilarations could not find expression in the intricate doctrines and trammeled practices of Anglican, Congregational, and Old Light Presbyterian traditions. Once again in American history a new way of being religious was in the making. The revivals of the turn of the century were more dramatic and more extensive than during the First Great Awakening. But rather than modifying existing church structures as it had in the First Great Awakening, revivalism in the Second Great Awakening led to organizing new religious groups.

Sociologists know that collective movements often develop under conditions of social strain. The demands of fighting a War for Independence temporarily resolved the fears, anxieties, and stress of large-scale social change. But when political peace came and there was no longer an external enemy to blame for all the problems and uncertainties, social strains reemerged—unmasked and with a vengeance. In addition to rapid economic fluctuations, the frustrations of children coming of age in a new society, and increased geographical mobility, Americans discovered more differences among themselves as they tried to form and administer political institutions. Joyous optimism about independence joined with a deep uneasiness about what it meant. Then from 1805 through 1812, the British again appeared to test the resolve of the fledgling nation. People wondered if the new nation would fulfill the promise of the Revolution. Social changes, political differences, and geographic diffusion made Americans uneasy. To find order, a developing nation needed cultural cohesion—a sense of common identity, with shared values, beliefs, and purposes. At this critical point, a new form of religion provided unifying experiences and goals.

Methodist and Baptist circuit-riders spread the good news of personal salvation through the isolated settlements of the frontier. Even with its emphasis on individual regeneration, the Second Great Awakening had the characteristics of a social movement. From a few converts, it expanded into a widespread organization of people in small groups all over America. The Awakening was led by a dedicated group of charismatic leaders who sought to reform the nation morally as well as spiritually. Their commitment to personal salvation and moral responsibility gave the movement clear goals, separating its members from the unsaved and offering criteria for Christian behavior. As the movement continued, a new, administrative group "routinized" the charisma, standardizing and institutionalizing what had once been spontaneous.

Looking at America at the turn of the nineteenth century, Donald G. Matthews observes that:

> the Revival in this general social strain promised a "positive outcome in an uncertain situation," for it proposed to make men better by putting them into direct contact with God. It also provided values or goals for which to work and codes which regulated behavior giving ideological as well as social order to life.

And Matthews concludes that:

> the measure of the success of the Awakening was not in the length of various periods of enthusiasm, however, even though many ministers of the time thought so. The measure was in the number of new churches organized which could persist when enthusiasm had died down, the number of converts who remained in the churches once their emotions had been channeled from public ecstasy into private devotion.[6]

Although Methodism was newly planted in America, the number of its "friends" increased from 10,500 in 1781 to 76,150 in 1791. In the Old Dominion, between 1790 and 1791, twenty thousand converts were swept into the Methodist fold in a single year. Methodists were able to accomplish such dramatic growth because they had an administrative hierarchy that oversaw the itinerant ministry of charismatic preachers. These traveling ministers did not wait for communities to form on the frontier or for "calls" from established churches. Instead, like professional organizers, they went straight to the people, moving from house to house, speaking directly to the people, in simple, moving language. After bringing a few converts together in a newly settled area, the Methodist evangelist would appoint one of them to lead the group, and then move on.

At first a tradition of radical congregational polity prevented Baptists from being so well organized. But soon Baptist preachers, like the Methodists, were delivering the message of salvation in ways to which the people could respond. They too organized many new churches. As they moved west, the Methodists tended to travel north and the Baptists south. "In a single ten-year period," says Matthews, "the combined strength of the two popular denominations jumped from 45,000 to 121,000."[7] Soon an entirely new group, the Disciples of Christ—uniting schismatic Methodists, Baptists, and evangelical Presbyterians—came to life on the frontier and joined the others in seizing the religious leadership of the new nation from the Eastern churches.

Along with rapid numerical growth came a new concept of the church. As an organic part of a traditional community, the church's previous role had emphasized maintaining spiritual and moral order. The circuit-riders, though, were organizing groups of people with changed lives, people who were intent on changing the lives and character of entire communities. This new, purposive idea of the church was the heart of a social movement. The form of the institution was new, but its spiritual impetus was not altogether novel. The Puritans sought to build "a citty vpon a hill"; now the evangelical preachers planted churches on the frontier. Methodists, Baptists, and Disciples led the movement, and Congregationalists and Presbyterians organized hundreds of missionary and benevolent societies. Action on the frontier affected the organization of established churches in the East. Denominationalism gave a new institutional shape to a renewed "errand into the wilderness." Eventually its new form altered the purpose of the original mission beyond recognition.

Since the movement relied largely on people to manage their own religious affairs it had a democratizing influence. The movement, as T. Scott Miyakawa has shown, was also an important nationalizing force. By multiplying similar church groups throughout the nation, the movement helped people far apart geographically to share common values, ideas, and commitments. Together with increasing economic interaction and growing national political involvement, the denominational movement helped create a cohesive American culture, as opposed to a grouping of distinct provinces. The resulting world of common experience existed through literally thousands of local church organizations. Matthews aptly concludes:

> The pulsation of organization and movement—order and mission—persisted for about fifty years. After the early 1790s the Awakening became more general, affecting each section of the new nation with its values and language until all America seemed to have become a "revivalistic" society: a community quickened by appeals to mission, ordered by reproaches of sin and saved by personal exertion in doing good and doing well. This accomplishment was made possible by the persistent combination of social strain, ecclesiastical turmoil and purposive leadership. Because of the ubiquity of the latter and the flexibility of their appeal, the Awakening provided something for everyone. There was orderly benevolence for those in the older churches, a stimulating emotional catharsis for others. There was the *promise* of perfection for some, and the *example* of it for the more sanguine.[8]

Local church organizations at the heart of this social movement were accepted by Americans—no matter what their theological stripe or European background—as the norm for the nation's religious institutions.

Protestant denominationalism is a distinctly American creation. In the words of Kenneth Scott Latourette, "the Christianity which developed in the United States [after 1800] was unique. It displayed features which marked it as distinct from previous Christianity in any other land."[9] Historian Sidney E. Mead has catalogued the basic elements, ideas, and practices of American denominational institutions. He notes that American denominations tend to justify their beliefs and behavior by denying their recent history and claiming to conform to the concept of the church as set forth in the New Testament. Because their membership was based on freely given consent, rather than political coercion, American religious groups became voluntary associations, independent of the state.

Along with the denomination's antihistorical bias and voluntaryism, there was an emphasis on missionary enterprise. Commitment to missions has often energized competition between churches, but this impetus also provided a basis for an awareness of broader Christian purposes and a platform for interdenominational cooperation. Since the Puritans, a common sense of mission has characterized American religious life. Mead observes that revivalism, with its stress on personal conversions, became more than a technique for recruitment—charismatic leaders sought practical results, used popular language, downplayed Christian nurture, and stimulated anti-intellectual bias among American Protestants.

Perhaps reacting against the Enlightenment, American churches at this time stressed inner spiritual experience far more than rational theology as the basis of faith. Despite the values and commitments they shared, there was rivalry among the denominations. Competition was sometimes keen and Mead found "sardonic jealousy reflected in the reputed remark of the Baptist revivalist who in commenting on his meetings said, 'We won only two last night, but thank God the Methodists across the street did not win any!' "[10] However, competitive efforts were often good-natured and cooperative.

With these characteristics in mind, we should be more able to understand what H. Richard Niebuhr calls "the social sources of denominationalism"—those developing social traits that help to explain the dramatic rise and continuing influence of these religious institutions in the United States. If one looks at the distinctive ideas they profess, one sees a wide variety of religious groups in America. But ideas do not exist in a vacuum. Indeed, as Niebuhr points out, theological opinions grow from the relations between a group's religion and other social, or political, institutions. Hence sociology may help the historian of religious institutions to distinguish surface differences from basic similarities.

Drawing upon the work of Max Weber and Ernst Troeltsch, Niebuhr observes that one who studies religious institutions must distinguish between the "church" and the "sect." Essentially, the church is "a natural social group akin to the family or the nation," while the sect is "a voluntary association." More precisely, as Niebuhr writes, this means:

> members are born into the church while they must join the sect. Churches are inclusive institutions, frequently national in scope, and emphasize the universalism of the gospel; while sects are exclusive in character, appeal to the individualistic element in Christianity, and emphasize its ethical demands. Membership in a church is socially obligatory, the necessary consequence of birth into a family or nation, and no special requirements condition its privileges; the sect, on the other hand, is likely to demand some definite type of religious experience as a pre-requisite of membership.
>
> These differences in structure have their corollaries in differences in ethics and doctrine.[11]

Sects usually begin as minority movements. With the passage of generations, an increase in wealth often follows upon the asceticism of the sect and membership grows because of its successful missionary activity. When wealth and numbers bring increasing involvement in the nation's economic and political life, the sect often becomes a church.

Religious freedom gave all the religious groups in the United States the political status of sects. And the frontier provided a social environment conducive to revivalistic spiritual experiences and the spread of voluntary religious associations. Group more sectarian in cast (for example, Methodists, Baptists, and Disciples of Christ) thrived in comparison to those that were "church-like" (that is, Presbyterians, Congregationalists, and Episcopalians). But as frontier communities passed from being pioneer outposts and became farming settlements and towns:

> the frontier sect becomes a rural church, in which the sharply defined character, inherited from the pioneer days, has been modified by the

influence of social habit. The bright colors are toned down. . . . The revival, losing its spontaneous character, becomes a ritual form—a method on which the church and the unredeemed children of converted parents can rely for the desired results. Conversion is regularly expected and occurs with an almost equal regularity. The sectarian organization takes on a churchly aspect, providing means of education in Sunday Schools and other agencies, whereby the second and third generations may be instructed in the ways of the fathers. Creeds, whether written or unwritten, become increasingly important as symbols of social unity and social differentiation. Piety remains directed primarily to the salvation of the soul, yet the gain of less spiritual but none the less desired goods of economic and communal life is also its object.

And then, says Niebuhr:

When the frontier faith becomes domesticated in this way in the rural church, it does not thereby enter into closer relationship with the religion of the older settlements. The latter has in the meantime become urban in character, if it was not so to begin with. Friction between metropolis and farm is substituted for the conflict between established settlement and frontier.

As these differences become ingrained by habit and culture, Niebuhr concludes, "East and West remain divided by different thought-forms and attitudes nurtured by commercial, metropolitan life and by agricultural economics."[12]

While sects tended to become churches, churches remained divided along sectional lines between East and West and, bolstered by racial discrimination, between North and South. As a Christian, Niebuhr wants to reconcile these differences, and makes some theological proposals for church unity. Yet his most telling point remains his description of how religious institutions are involved with, and influenced by, economic and social conditions. His approach is based on Max Weber's famous thesis on the interconnections of the Protestant Reformation and the rise of bourgeois capitalism. Accidental events, like the appearance of Calvin in Geneva, and coincidental factors, like the ease of communication between developing commercial centers, may account for the original association between the new faith and the new commercial classes. But Weber saw more rational causes strengthening the association throughout the centuries. Calvinism's strong sense of vocation—with God calling the individual to a certain kind of life—coincided with the moral and religious interests of the bourgeoisie. And Calvinism nurtured the very virtues—individual responsibility, thriftiness, and deferred gratification—that made the growth of trade and the rise of the bourgeoisie possible. Then, too, by concentrating on certain teachings and minimizing others, the rising economic group successfully modified religion to meet its desires.

As a historian, Niebuhr knows that "it remained for America to carry the accommodation of the faith to bourgeois psychology to its extremes." And this vexes him because, in his judgment:

> Here the comfortable circumstances of an established economic class have simplified out of existence the problem of evil and have made possible the substitution for the mysterious will of the Sovereign of life and death and sin and salvation, the sweet benevolence of a Father-Mother God or the vague goodness of the All. . . . This is not the religion of that middle class which struggled with kings and popes in defense of its economic and religious liberties but the religion of a bourgeoisie whose conflicts are over and which has passed into the quiet waters of assured income and established social standing.[13]

With his passion for social justice and his vision of Christian unity, Niebuhr's ire doubtless was justified. But we should not let the appeal of his sarcasm undercut his perceptive discussion of the close relations between denominational religious institutions and their social and economic background.

In fact, because this close relationship persists, one could argue that all religious groups, not only Protestants, even not only Christians, have become institutionalized as denominations in the United States. One need only recall Mead's summary of the salient characteristics:

> Religious freedom and the challenge of the frontier's unchurched shaped certain colonial religious patterns into the structure we recognize as American denominationalism. . . . competition, made keen in an environment of freedom, has promoted revivalism as a technique, voluntaryism as a cohesive base, and historylessness as a cast

of mind. Withal has come an anti-intellectual bias and a sense of purposive enterprise which is peculiarly reflective of the nineteenth-century American society in which the Protestant denominations throve.[14]

With these basic elements in mind, one can claim that becoming "Protestant" in this way is the price of survival in America for religious groups—Catholics, Jews, and others.

Religious freedom, then, has an ironic twist: by freeing religious groups to be themselves, the separation of church and state has actually imposed upon them all the "equality" of sameness. Despite differences of doctrine and despite varieties of ethnic heritage, all religious groups in the United States have tended to take on the social structure of denominationalism. To the Enlightened framers of the Constitution, each religion was valuable insofar as it contributed to civic virtue, the necessary undergirding of the nation. In practice, this means that differences of belief among religious groups have become increasingly irrelevant to their place in American society, while otherwise diverse religious groups are considered valuable because—in some vague way—they "make good citizens" and "strengthen the moral fiber of the nation."

The obvious shortcoming here is that theology is increasingly unnecessary to the life of religious institutions. Doctrinal beliefs become matters of opinion which figure less and less prominently in an individual's choice of churches or church programs. Social class, liturgical style, and moral tone replace doctrine as ways of characterizing churches. In later chapters, we will see that the most creative religious thinking was often done outside the churches. Yet the structural sameness of religious institutions has enabled many groups to be accepted into the mainstream of American life as denominations. Sometimes it took several generations, but for many immigrants—and who other than the Indian is not immigrant in America?—denominational religious institutions eased the strains of acculturation.

The social structure of religious institutions was an agent of coexistence and relatively peaceful change, but denominational Protestantism was not uniformly benign. Following the Second Great Awakening, as frontier sects became churches, the Protestant denominations began to form what Martin Marty calls "the righteous empire"—a powerful network of purposive voluntary associations. The "empire" was sometimes charitable and benevolent, sometimes viciously discriminatory and imperialistic. Denominational Protestantism supplied a shared language and common values for the developing nation. Concomitantly it legitimated many good and bad aspects of American life.

As a kind of institution, denominational Protestantism played an essential role in national development in the early nineteenth century. Yet even the immigrants the empire excluded were entering the middle class, and new immigrants were steadily arriving. After the Civil War, industrialization and urbanization joined immigration as social forces tearing at the fabric of "the righteous empire." When moral and intellectual changes also began to multiply, the empire began to crumble. But this did not destroy denominationalism. The institutional structure of denominationalism had become so habitually ingrained in American religious consciousness that even "strangers" could become, in a sense, Protestants. About a century after the Second Great Awakening, and after considerable internal debate, Roman Catholics accepted their "Americanization" as *one*, rather than *the*, church in America. Roman Catholics in America have a revival tradition, and some Jews have Sunday schools. Zionism might be interpreted as a Jewish mission enterprise. These three faiths are now referred to as the major denominations. All three support the "religion" of the American way of life. Thus denominationalism provides the institutional background for the rest of the story of religion in American history. Later generations discovered new ways of being religious in America, but the legacy of the Second Great Awakening is still with us.

Institutional differentiation is part of the way traditional communities evolve into modern societies. Religious institutions, like denominationalism, develop alongside political and economic ones. By drawing upon and reforming elements from colonial days, denominations organized the collective aspects of religious experience into institutions that allowed believers to cope with the stress of broad social change in the nineteenth century. Yet if institutional differentiation legitimated and thereby eased the beginnings of modernization for most Americans, more sentient thinkers began to ponder other appropriate ways of being religious in that time.

Sociologist Thomas Luckmann has hypothesized that progressive institutional differentiation leads to the privatization of religious consciousness. The process of institutional specialization allows religion to coexist with other increasingly distinct public institutions, such as political and economic structures. But as other institutions—big government, and big business—wield increasing influence on one's public life, an individual may find that his or her religion, if it is to survive, becomes an internal, private affair. Even in one's own mind, religion may become compartmentalized and remote from the rest of life.

A person whose religious experience becomes increasingly subjective may be frustrated with the kind of religiousness institutionalized in denominationalism. If his or her spiritual quest is to continue, such a person may seek some radically new way of being religious. This latter condition is prevalent in our own time, and later we will explore current spiritual options. But there were many such seekers in the nineteenth century. Perhaps the most fully articulated alternative to denominationalism in that time was Transcendentalism. Ralph Waldo Emerson was the chief prophet of the religion of nature and the leader of those who found in imaginative literature a new form for the expression of religion.

NOTES

1. "A Short History of the Life of Barton W. Stone Written by Himself," in Rhodes Thompson, ed., *Voices from Cane Ridge* (St. Louis: Bethany Press, 1954), p. 68.

2. Sydney E. Ahlstrom, *A Religious History of the American People* (New Haven: Yale University Press, 1972), p. 433.

3. Stone, pp. 69-72.

4. Joachim Wach, *Sociology of Religion* (Chicago: The University of Chicago Press, 1944), p. 377.

5. Talcott Parsons, "Introduction," in Max Weber, *The Sociology of Religion* (Boston: Beacon Press, 1963; first edition, 1922), p. xx.

6. Donald G. Matthews, "The Second Great Awakening as an Organizing Process, 1780-1830: An Hypothesis," *American Quarterly* 21, no. 1 (Spring 1969): 34, 35-36.

7. Ibid., p. 37.

8. Ibid., p. 40.

9. Kenneth Scott Latourette, *A History of the Expansion of Christianity*, 7 vols. (New York: Harper and Brothers, 1937-1945), 4:424.

10. Sidney E. Mead, *The Lively Experiment: The Shaping of Christianity in America* (New York: Harper and Row, 1963), p. 132.

11. H. Richard Niebuhr, *The Social Sources of Denominationalism* (New York: The World Publishing Company, 1929), pp. 17-18.

12. Ibid., pp. 181-82.

13. Ibid., pp. 104-5.

14. Mead, *The Lively Experiment*, p. 133.

5

TRANSCENDENTALISM: THE RELIGION OF NATURE IN THE FORM OF LITERATURE

The second quarter of the nineteenth century was a time of extraordinary cultural ferment in America. Movements to reform individuals and to recast society came from churches, from interdenominational agencies, from lonely prophets, and from popular crusades without ties to institutional religion. Abolition, temperance, women's rights, and many areas of life were targets of earnest campaigns and vigorous crackpots. The West was opening wider, and being filled. Andrew Jackson's presidency gave an image of popular democracy to the federal government. Spiritual visionaries and philosophical clubs hatched utopian communities. Leaders and causes came and went. Some crusades prospered; others fizzled or fissioned in new directions.

Not all was changed. Despite rebellions, slavery continued to oppress the South. The West was being "won" only at tremendous physical and psychic cost—particularly to women. But in the commercial cities and towns of the Northeast, it was indeed a heady time. Victorious in the War of 1812, enjoying peace and relative prosperity, the new nation—especially in New England—felt the exuberance of its cultural adolescence.

Denominational churches met the religious needs of many Americans, mostly in the South and West. In New England, many churches were split between the spiritless logic chopping of "consistent Calvinists" and the staid intellectuality of established Unitarianism. But if institutional religion languished, New England's broader culture, outside the churches, was lively and exciting. Orestes A. Brownson, to take an extreme but not atypical example, picked up and tried on for size practically every alternative the time offered for spiritual self-definition. There was a wild democracy of spiritual options—ranging from Brownson's *final* recourse to the Roman faith to new visions like Joseph Smith's *Book of Mormon*. Nathaniel Hawthorne's *The Scarlett Letter*, in which Arthur Dimmesdale symbolizes the disintegration of "consistent Calvinism" and Hester Prynne the rise of Transcendentalism, suggests some of the transitions in New England during the period.

Ralph Waldo Emerson's ideas, career, and forms of expression show that he was as much a man of his time as he was a creator of a new way of being religious. Nature was the source of revelation for Emerson's religion, and imaginative literature was its organ of expression. He influenced creative contemporaries like Henry David Thoreau, Walt Whitman, Nathaniel Hawthorne, and Herman Melville. Emerson instructed Margaret Fuller's rising feminism, and his "vision" inspired Bronson Alcott's radical utopianism. His ideas about language and spirit worked their way into the more orthodox Protestantism of Horace Bushnell. Even the Roman Catholicism of Isaac Hecker was touched by the romantic metaphysics in Emerson's "system." His effect on the romantic Unitarian faith was shown in the career of Theodore Parker, in the rise of civil morality in the works of Richard Henry Dana, Jr., and in the work of Transcendentalist ministers, such as Octavius Brooks Frothingham. As Brooks Atkinson puts it, "What he said and wrote is still the gospel we most easily understand."[1] Though never a joiner himself, Emerson was the chief oracle of the movement that came to be called Transcendentalism. Both the religious message and the form of the movement were new.

Born in Boston in 1803, Ralph Waldo Emerson came from a long line of New England clergymen. After graduating from Harvard College, he taught school for several years before enrolling at Harvard Divinity School. He completed his education there in 1829, and he was ordained assistant pastor in Boston's prestigious Second Church, where his father had preached. Soon he became a full pastor. Even the liberality of Unitarian practices was too confining for Emerson's spirit, however, and he resigned in 1832. He told his congregation that he could no longer administer the sacrament of communion because he did not believe that Christ had meant it to be a regular observance. Although the young minister was popular, his people could not go that far. Still, the resignation was amicable, and, in the future, Emerson would occasionally speak in churches, even if most of his "preaching" was in a new mode.

Disrupted in his career and upset by the death of his young wife, Emerson traveled to Europe, where he met Wordsworth, Coleridge, and Carlyle. The trip was a tonic, and Emerson returned to America restored, bought a house and land in Concord, remarried, and began his long career as a minister without a church—through essays, addresses, and poems. Some of his audiences were shocked, some troubled, many inspired, but practically no one was untouched. Because he articulated the spiritual yearnings of many of his contemporaries, his influence was immense. As Herman Melville, who heard Emerson speak on at least one occasion, put it, "Say what they will, he's a great man."[2] The heart of Emerson's gospel and its form of expression were, in his vision, organically related. Some of his ideas were modified slightly over the nearly fifty years of his career, but the essentials were remarkably present from the outset. His early essay *Nature*, in 1836, says it all.

In the 1842 edition of *Nature*, Emerson replaced an earlier quotation from Plotinus with a poem of his own as epigraph. Emerson's poems often do not read well by themselves, but many—like this one—introduce or summarize ideas for an essay:

A subtle chain of countless rings
The next unto the farthest brings;
The eye reads omens where it goes,
And speaks all languages the rose;
And, striving to be man, the worm
Mounts through all the spires of form.[3]

The revelatory, interconnected process of nature speaks to all men.

Emerson urges his "retrospective" age to hear its voice:

> The foregoing generations beheld God and nature face to face; we,
> through their eyes. Why should not we also enjoy an original rela-
> tion to the universe? Why should not we have a poetry and philos-
> ophy of insight and not of tradition, and a religion by revelation to
> us, and not the history of theirs? The sun shines to-day also. . . . Let
> us demand our own works and laws and worship.[4]

Here is our cultural Declaration of Independence. Emerson found
Americans living in a new land but still thinking, believing, acting,
and writing in old ways. Although they were free politically, he
saw his contemporaries in bondage to established traditions of
mind and spirit. Happily, no large struggle was required. To enjoy
experiences commensurate with their possibilities, Emerson said,
Americans need only investigate—with open eyes—their relation
to nature.

An intimate, potentially religious relationship with nature is a
mode of spirituality especially appropriate for Americans. Indeed
the hazards and wonder of the natural world soon altered the religious heritage immigrating Americans brought from Europe. But
Emerson was concerned with something more than the natural environment. He wanted to differentiate and also connect two basic
realities: Nature and the Soul. See how much his definition of Nature encompasses: "Strictly speaking, therefore, all that is separate
from us, all which Philosophy distinguishes as the NOT-ME, that
is, both nature and art, all other men and my own body, must be
ranked under the same NATURE."[5] So generously conceived, Nature is the place for man's highest spiritual experiences, for those
religious exhilarations that transcend the confines of tradition-
bound churches.

Presaging perhaps Rudolf Otto's definition of "the idea of the
holy" as a conjoint sense of *tremendum* (awe, fear, majesty) and
fascinans (attraction, joy, exuberance), Emerson says, in Nature "I
am glad to the brink of fear."[6] Such classic religious feelings come
forth in Nature because it includes everything other than one's own
soul. Hence, when a person is in Nature, "all mean egotism van-
ishes. I become a transparent eyeball; I am nothing; I see all; the

currents of Universal Being circulate through me; I am part or parcel of God."[7] Eyesight is Emerson's favorite image for revelation because the eyes are our organs of most immediate perception, unsullied by conventions of language or consciousness informed by tradition. In this sense, vision was the chief metaphor of Transcendentalism—the eye makes the passage between the Soul and Nature. Clarity of vision is how one gains "an original relation to the universe." Students of Transcendentalism, especially after reading Hawthorne or Melville, often detect a certain naiveté or innocence in Emerson's stress on vision as a channel of religion. Yet, even in 1836, Emerson's espousal of a visionary relationship with Nature was anything but simplistic.

The main portion of Emerson's essay *Nature* elaborates various "uses" of nature for the eyes of man. First and most obvious is "commodity," those products derived by reproducing or recombining natural processes—from corn to railroads. The second, more complex use of nature is "beauty," including (1) the delight one finds in the simple perception of natural forms, (2) the sense of a higher, spiritual element infusing noble, heroic actions, and (3) the intellectual apprehension of "the absolute order of things as they stand in the mind of God." Taking these three aspects of beauty together, "the creation of beauty is Art." So "a work of art is an abstract or epitome of the world," and "the standard of beauty is the entire circuit of natural forms—the totality of nature."[8] Yet, in Emerson's view, even art is penultimate, for "beauty in nature . . . is the herald of inward and eternal beauty, and is not alone a solid and satisfactory good. It must stand as a part, and not yet as the last or highest expression of the final cause of Nature."[9] Commodity and beauty lead beyond their own utility, toward even higher ends.

Emerson provides the best clues to the character of his own religious vocation in his discussion of language as "a third use which Nature subserves to man." Here his remarkable compression demonstrates long concentration, as he writes:

> Nature is the vehicle of thought, and in a simple, double, and three-fold degree.
> 1. Words are signs of natural facts.

    2. Particular natural facts are symbols of particular spiritual facts.

    3. Nature is the symbol of spirit.[10]

Study of this syllogism shows that language actually expresses and embodies spiritual reality. Words originally come into being as emblems of natural facts; moreover, "every natural fact is a symbol of some spiritual fact." Observing Nature, "man is conscious of a universal soul within or behind his individual life. . . . This universal soul he calls Reason: It is not mine, or thine, or his, but we are its. . . . That which intellectually considered we call Reason, considered in relation to Nature we call Spirit. Spirit is the Creator. Spirit hath life in itself."[11]

Even when tradition and convention make language degenerate, "wise men pierce this rotten diction and fasten words again to visible things; so that picturesque language is at once a commanding certificate that he who employs it is a man in alliance with truth and God. . . . Hence, good writing and brilliant discourse are perpetual allegories."[12] The religious significance of language is clinched by Emerson's belief that the world itself—everything that Emerson means by "Nature," everything that is the "NOT-ME"—is actually emblematic of spiritual reality. So language is the vehicle for the spiritual reality the open eye perceives in Nature. Emerson is convinced that "this relation between the mind and matter is not fancied by some poet, but stands in the will of God, and so is free to be known by all men."[13] Thus language has religious import also by expressing a natural spiritual democracy.

The conviction of a deep correspondence between the world of material nature and the reality of spirit—an important legacy of Puritanism—was widespread in Emerson's time. Indeed it was perhaps the main assumption relating Americans of otherwise diverse religious inclinations. Like many of his cosmopolitan contemporaries, Emerson found the doctrine of correspondence interpreted persuasively in the writings of that eccentric mystic-scientist, Emmanuel Swedenborg. Yet however widely shared and, for many, an unconscious presupposition of all thought, the doctrine of correspondence did not go unexamined. For example, Thoreau, Hawthorne, and Melville tested this central tenet of the vision

Emerson was articulating for so many Americans. Emerson saw clearly what remarkable power the doctrine of correspondence invested in the language of literature. Hence Emerson adumbrates some of the close connections between religion and imaginative literature.

If language shows how "the world shall be to us an open book," Nature's ultimate lesson is what Emerson calls discipline. Discipline includes commodity, beauty, and language "as parts of itself." Discipline works in two ways. First, "the understanding adds, divides, combines, measures, and finds nutriment and room for its activity" in the "worthy scene" of "space, time, society, labor, climate, food, locomotion, the animals, [and] the mechanical forces." The "understanding" operates in scientific, commercial, and social life, teaching all the lessons of power and empowering all the exercises of man's will. Then, second, "meantime, Reason transfers all these lessons into its own world of thought, by perceiving the analogy that marries Nature and Mind."[14] Reason perceives the infinite unity of all things; words express it, actions "publish" and perfect it. Concluding the central message of Nature, Emerson writes, "Thus is the unspeakable but intelligible and practicable meaning of the world conveyed to man, the immortal pupil [student and eye], in every object of sense. To this one end of Discipline, all parts of nature conspire."[15] A century earlier, Jonathan Edwards found Christian practice the soundest measure of authentic religious affections; Emerson's emphasis on discipline as the highest use of nature keeps the pragmatic side of the Puritan legacy alive by making it new.

Although "motion, poetry, physical and intellectual science, and religion, all tend to affect our convictions of the reality of the external world,"[16] Emerson found idealism—the notion that matter is unreal and that the spirit only is real—finally unsatisfactory. Construing a notion of "immanence" that resides at the heart of the metaphysics of his time, Emerson's view—coalescing the epistemic idealism of an Edwards with the empiricism of a Franklin—is more unified:

> Behind nature, throughout nature, spirit is present; one and not compound it does not act upon us from without, that is, in space or time, but spiritually, or through ourselves: therefore [we learn] that spirit,

that is, the Supreme Being, does not build up nature around us, but puts it forth through us, as the life of the tree puts forth new branches and leaves through the pores of the old. As a plant upon the earth, so a man rests upon the bosom of God; he is nourished by unfailing fountains, and draws at his need inexhaustible power. Who can set bounds to the possibilities of man?[17]

The "prospects" are good for the man who knows that "his relation to the world . . . is arrived at by untaught sallies of the spirit, by a continual self-recovery, and by entire humility."[18]

Inheriting its obsession with perfection or spiritual "completion," Transcendentalism in effect revived the old Puritan experiment and applied its principles of discipline and aspiration to new frontiers of consciousness within the individual self. Mixing his own words with sayings attributed to "a certain Orphic poet," Emerson ends the essay by speaking directly to his contemporaries:

> The problem of restoring to the world original and eternal beauty is solved by the redemption of the soul. The ruin or the blank that we see when we look at nature, is in our own eye. . . . The reason why the world lacks unity, and lies broken and in heaps, is because man is disunited with himself. He cannot be a naturalist until he satisfies all the demands of the spirit. Love is as much its demand as perception. Indeed, neither can be perfect without the other . . .
>   . . . You also are a man. . . .
>   . . . Every spirit builds itself a house, and beyond its house a world, and beyond its world a heaven. Know then that the world exists for you. For you is the phenomenon perfect. What we are, that only we can see. All that Adam had, all that Caesar could, you have and can do. . . .Build therefore your own world. As fast as you conform your life to the pure idea in your mind, that will unfold its great proportions. A correspondent revolution in things will attend the influx of spirit . . . until evil is no more seen. The kingdom of man over nature, which cometh not with observation—a dominion such as now is beyond his dream of God—he shall enter without more wonder than the blind man feels who is gradually returned to sight.[19]

The fact that such a sophisticated essay ends so directly—concluding with an "altar call" as did the sermons of the revivalists—suggests that Emerson is both philosopher and preacher. In some ways Transcendentalism was the revivalism of an educated elite. Because he saw language as a natural vehicle of spirit, Emerson's form was the literary address or essay. But his carefully fashioned sentences have a direction beyond their words. He wanted his language to open the eyes of his audience to see the world afresh and express its meaning in their own words. Then his hearers and readers would be liberated from the constraints of tradition, free to discover their own ways of being religious.

Henry James wrote appreciatively of Emerson that "life never bribed him to look at anything but the soul." In this sense, it is fair to think of Emerson as a psychologist. Whatever his subject—the American scholar, the poet, the transcendentalist, experience, self-reliance, heroism, the conduct of life—the goal of his writing was always the same: to use language to revitalize the souls of those who heard his words. He wanted to convert people from old visions and restore them to themselves. Here was a genuinely new way of being religious in America.

Emerson was not a joiner. He did not seek disciples, nor found a sect or church. He did not want "satellites." He was free, and he wanted other people to be free to discover their own "orbits," to cut new spiritual paths. So it is difficult to gauge the effect of his message in numerical terms. Certainly his vision was poorly reflected by any who might call themselves "Emersonians." But it easy to see Emerson's impact where we may most appropriately seek it—in the literary works of his contemporaries and successors who sought to plumb the religious meanings of American life. Emerson spoke so directly for a new kind of American consciousness that his message was unavoidable. The power of his vision is revealed most clearly perhaps in the works of those who adopted his method or form— the language of imaginative literature—to test the sufficiency of his main convictions.

The study of imaginative literature is an important resource for the cultural study of religion. Paul Tillich's aphorism—"Religion is the substance of culture; culture the form of religion"—suggests that the study of cultural forms such as imaginative literature gives access to the sometimes unconscious values that shape and support a society. Literary images, symbols, and actions often express the ways religious beliefs and values come to life. Because a work of imaginative literature can show what kinds of thought and behavior grow from certain convictions, the work may also serve to examine religious beliefs, or even to call them into question by portraying their unperceived experiential consequences. Nathan A. Scott, Jr., observed that works of literature may be of great service to the theologian. Giles Gunn, Wesley Kort, and Robert Detweiler, among others, have explored a variety of relations between religion and imaginative literature.[20] Emerson's work deserves reappraisal in this context, for he shows how uncontrived relations are between nature, language, and spirit. His *Nature* essay demonstrates the significance of these natural ties for interpreters of American life.

The natural environment provides a ready symbol for all those aspects of the "NOT-ME" that, by their revelatory otherness, awaken the soul to know itself. For the Transcendentalists, nature symbolized a new life beyond the confines of old selves. Because words began as signs of natural facts, language had the potential for expressing the spiritual glory of nature. A fresh and imaginative use of language, then, could make the religious possibilities of nature available even to Americans residing in prosperous towns and cities far from the actual frontier. Emerson rightly divined the worth of imaginative uses of language in America, and several of his contemporaries were quick to press beyond his prophetic achievements. What Emerson saw and said in addresses, essays, and poems, writers such as Thoreau and Melville began to invest in the forms of fiction.

Thoreau's *Walden* and Melville's *Moby-Dick* illustrate Emerson's purposes because the authors provided sufficient space and time to create an entire world of experience—fulfilling Emerson's imperative to "build therefore your own world." Inviting the reader into the world of his characters' experience, the writer also gives the reader an opportunity to test the validity of Emerson's vision of nature. By referring to his own beliefs and values, the reader can judge the relevance and truth of the writer's vision. In several ways, then, imaginative literature leads into religious concerns. In particular, Emerson's vision of nature and the role of language opens a whole field of resources for the cultural study of religion in America.

Even the naive reader who misses much of the author's art recognizes that Emerson's vision of nature was Thoreau's guiding inspiration. By using his own experiencing self as the hero of his story, and by imagining a natural narrative sequence for the self's coming to terms with the "NOT-ME," Thoreau as a writer gives the readers of *Walden* the possibility of spiritual renewal that Emerson so often essayed. Thoreau examines Emerson's ideas about language and nature in an artfully imagined experience, and *Walden* ends primarily by affirming Emerson's vision.

A more full-fledged fictional evaluation of Emerson's views is found in Melville's *Moby-Dick*. Melville was deeply attuned to his age's desire to achieve the personal and cultural freedom of what Emerson called "an original relation to the universe." And he was aware of the great promise of Emerson's proposal of "mounting through all the spires of form" to reach this goal. But Melville's Dutch Reformed background made him hesitate to embrace such sunny propositions without question; his writing became a way of imaginatively testing their plausibility in the hypothetical or virtual realm of fiction. This process of testing tended to confirm his suspicions and led him, therefore, to complicate Emerson's view. In pursuing these complications, Melville developed his own vision of the religious import of the self's relation to nature.

Melville structured *Moby-Dick* along the lines of two vastly different yet inextricably united stories—the tragedy of Captain Ahab and the eventual redemption of the narrator, Ishmael. Feeling depressed, Ishmael goes to sea, inadvertently joining Ahab's quest for revenge on the white whale who has taken his leg and wounded his pride. Ishamael gradually extricates himself from Ahab's quest, as Ahab is increasingly consumed by it. Ahab dominates his crew the way he seeks to rule the natural world; in the end, only Ishmael survives.

In the story of Ahab, Melville examines the dark side of the Transcendentalists' ideal of freedom. Above all, Ahab desires to be free, to name the universe for himself. Melville portrays Ahab's incredible desire for life as a monomania for independence. But, like other American heroes—such as Fitzgerald's Gatsby and Faulkner's Sutpen—Ahab falls into the chasm between appearance and reality. His monomania obscures from him the knowledge that life involves change, that life is fluid, organic, and always vital. When Ahab tries to make reality correspond to his vision, he is destroyed, because such an attempt necessarily involves the transgression of the natural bounds and social limits of human existence. Ahab mentally compresses all evil into the personified Moby-Dick:

> All evil, to crazy Ahab, [was] visibly personified, and made practically assailable in Moby Dick. He piled upon the whale's white hump the sum of all the general rage and hate felt by his whole race from Adam down; and then, as if his chest had been a mortar, he burst his hot heart's shell upon it.[21]

Ahab is mad not because he believes there is a real evil and maliciousness rampant in the universe, but rather because he thinks he can attack and defeat it in a single, all-inclusive incarnation.

Ahab's monomania narrows him and removes him from human concerns. He berates the gods for creating and then abandoning the little cabin boy, Pip, and swears that he, Ahab, will do better. However, he ends by doing worse, for he follows revenge instead of love. Ahab is unwilling to receive the wisdom that Pip brings from his near-death beneath the sea. Ahab also rejects first mate Starbuck's prudent advice, as he turns away from the vision of home and humanity he sees in Starbuck's eyes. Both Pip and Starbuck call him back to the human and the concrete, but Ahab's humanities do not win out, and he is angered further when he is tempted to accede to them. So Ahab moves steadily away from human sociality, toward increasing isolation. Hardening his heart, Ahab takes on the values of the head, of which the Parsee harpooner, Fedallah, is the extreme representative. Fedallah lures Ahab toward the Manichaeanism of seeing things as totally good or totally evil and away from a sense of human mediations and mitigations. Thus Ahab's search for the white whale becomes a Faustian quest of the human against the divine, an attempt to impose a man's will upon nature.

Ahab is propelled beyond any sort of reverence toward defiance. Defying the gods, Ahab also turns away from his fellow men. In his Promethean rage against the mocking of the gods—and who besides mad Pip has known their mocking as has Ahab?—he insists on the full humanity of his being, but rejects a sense of the inter-indebtedness of men. He is, indeed, "a grand, ungodly, god-like man." When the corpusants dance on the yardarms, Ahab offers to worship the gods in reverence if they will come to him in and on his own terms. After realizing they will not, he seizes upon defiance as the only true form of worship. He is blasphemous as he attempts to blow out the last fear, and his blasphemy is compounded by the willful isolation of his attempt. As Ahab replies to one of Starbuck's calming entreaties, "Talk not to me of blasphemy, man; I'd strike the sun if it insulted me."[22] Ahab's isolation from his fellow-men and against the gods has ungodly consequences for himself and the rest of the men, except Ishmael, whose response to experience provides an alternative to Ahab's independent fury.

In contrast to the single-minded Ahab, Ishmael is a pluralist. In telling his story, he uses many guises and reversals, alternating between comedy and dread, to show the shifting distinctions between laughter and woe. As an actor in the story he recounts, Ishmael does not begin this way. He enters as a willful, though humorous, outcast and *isolato* who joins the others in pledging themselves to Ahab's quest. Ishmael's progression from misanthropy to acceptance, and from a single view to a sense of perspective is marked by repeated epiphanies, in which he learns to reject finally both Ahab's tragic and isolated monomania and also its opposite, a sunny and pantheistic vision of all existence.

Ishmael moves toward comradeship, sociality, trust, love, and acceptance—the values of the heart—of which the pagan harpooner Queequeg is the extreme representative. Ishmael also becomes more questioning than Ahab; Ishmael questions not only the meaning of natural symbols but also the nature of the symbolizing process itself. He questions how man can know more rigorously than Ahab does. Ishmael's epistemological curiosity and humility conjoin with a series of events that develop the possibility of his final deliverance. His redemptive relationship with Queequeg gives him insights into human interdependence in the "Monkey-Rope" chapter. Ishmael's experiences with the wonders of nature and the comradeship of men help him to acknowledge Ahab's convictions while recognizing they do not go far enough. Ishmael survives in an isolation that brings him back to humanity. He is finally delivered to live again in the world of his experience, to re-create it, and to make it available to others by telling it, to share it and thus to humanize it.

As shown in his review of Hawthorne's "Mosses" and in the complementary sermons of Father Mapple and the cook in *Moby-Dick*, Melville saw truth-speaking as a religious duty. Ishmael demonstrates that truth-seeking must be relentless; although it may be ambiguous, it remains the truth. To Melville it is the values of the heart, brought to definition and fullness through being tested by the values of the head, that enable an individual to seek the truth, to speak the truth, and thereby achieve full identity.

What happens in the book is complex. The lessons Ishmael learns aboard the Pequod open his eyes to the diversities of nature. The symbolic whale is both malicious and benign, available for confrontation and beyond possession. The rewards of Ishmael's experience are the insights of his story. The product of his experience is the new self we know as the narrator. By virtue of his encounter with nature (all that is the "NOT-ME"), Ishmael gains a new sense of harmony with the natural world, an identification with the crew on board, and a new sense of brotherhood with the savage Queequeg. These realizations bring about his deliverance as a character at the end of the tale—buoyed up by Queequeg's coffin—and sustain his delivery to us of the experience itself.

By using the language of imaginative literature in *Moby-Dick* to investigate and complicate Emerson's vision of the religion of nature, Melville points the direction for the major impact of Trancendentalism on American culture. American literature continued to be a possible form for the expression of religion. Yet even in literature, as in social life, things soon become too darkly complicated for Transcendentalism to shine clearly or to contribute directly to American culture. Although Emerson was far from simple-minded, the Civil War and the failure of Reconstruction made his vision appear simplistic. As Henry James wrote in his biography of Hawthorne in 1879:

> The subsidence of that great convulsion has left a different tone from the tone it found, and one may say that the . . . war marks an era in the history of the American mind. It introduced into the national consciousness a certain sense of proportion and relation, of the world being a more complicated place than it had hitherto seemed, the future more treacherous, success more difficult. At the rate at which things are going, it is obvious that good Americans will be more numerous than ever; but the good American, in days to come, will be a more critical person than his complacent and confident grandfather. . . . He will not, I think, be a skeptic, and still less, of course, a cynic; but he will be, without discredit to his well-known capacity for action, an observer. He will remember that the ways of the Lord are inscrutable, and that this is a world in which everything happens; and eventualities will not find him intellectually unprepared.[23]

If he was too optimistic about the lessons learned, James was nevertheless right about the magnitude of the changes. Survivors of the Civil War and people coming of age in what Mark Twain aptly dubbed "the Gilded Age" needed a new way of being religious, for social changes required something more robust than the religion of nature. An active concern with social justice was the religious order of the new day.

NOTES

1. Brooks Atkinson, ed., *The Selected Writings of Ralph Waldo Emerson* (New York: The Modern Library, 1964), p. xxv.

2. Jay Leyda, ed., *The Melville Log* (New York: Godwin Press, 1969), Vol. I, p. 287.

3. Atkinson, *The Selected Writings of Emerson*, p. 2.

4. Ibid., p. 3.

5. Ibid., p. 4.

6. Ibid., p. 6.

7. Ibid.

8. Ibid., p. 13.

9. Ibid., p. 14.

10. Ibid.

11. Ibid., p. 15.

12. Ibid., p. 17.

13. Ibid., p. 19.

14. Ibid., p. 20.

15. Ibid., p. 26.

16. Ibid., p. 33.

17. Ibid., p. 35.

18. Ibid., p. 37.

19. Ibid., pp. 41-42.

20. See Nathan A. Scott, Jr., ed., *The New Orpheus: Essays Toward a Christian Poetic* (New York: Sheed and Ward, 1964), and *The Broken Center: Studies in the Theological Horizon of Modern Literature* (New Haven: Yale University Press, 1966); Giles Gunn, ed., *Literature and Religion* (London: SCM Press, Ltd., 1971); Wesley A. Kort, *Narrative Elements and Religious Meanings* (Philadelphia: Fortress Press, 1975); and Robert Detweiler, *Story, Sign, and Self: Phenomenology and Structuralism as Literary-Critical Methods* (Philadelphia: Fortress Press, 1978).

21. Herman Melville, *Moby-Dick; or The Whale* (Indianapolis: Bobbs-Merrill, Inc., 1964), p. 247 [chapter 41].

22. Ibid., p. 221 [chapter 36].

23. Henry James, *Hawthorne* (Ithaca: Cornell University Press, 1966), p. 114.

6

ETHOS AND ETHICS IN THE GILDED AGE

In 1873 Mark Twain and Charles Dudley Warner called the post-Reconstruction era "the Gilded Age." Because of its aptness, the label stuck. Historian Richard Hofstadter summarizes the period:

> For a generation after the Civil War, a time of great economic exploitation and waste, grave social corruption and ugliness, the dominant note in American political life was complacency. Although dissenting minorities were always present, they were submerged by the overwhelming realities of industrial growth and continental settlement.[1]

Steadily increasing industrialization, rapid urbanization, mounting immigration, and economic fluctuations combined with the trauma of the Civil War and the frustrations of Reconstruction to make Americans uneasy. The role of religion was ambiguous. On the one hand, many churchmen felt called to mediate traditional sacred symbols in order to sanction the energies of the captains of industry and to soothe the protective complacency of the bourgeoisie. On the other hand, many religious thinkers and activists felt equally called to challenge the moral ideas and practices of the dominant classes. The Gilded Age experienced a dissonance between its ethos and its ethics that has continued, for good or ill, to characterize religion in American life.

If culture is the web of meanings through which humans have personal and social being, then religion may be understood as the way people symbolically express their culture's relation to a primordial, fundamental order of reality, often imaged as a divine being. Anthropologist Clifford Geertz analyzes the role of religion in culture by looking at how "sacred symbols function to synthesize a people's ethos—the tone, character, and quality of their life, its moral and aesthetic style and mood—and their world view—the picture they have of the way things in sheer actuality are, their most comprehensive ideas of order."[2] A "healthy" culture might be defined as one that responds creatively to the junction, or disjunction, between its ethos and its world view. If these two aspects of life were generally out of alignment during the Gilded Age, there were at least two creative ethical responses.

Sidney E. Mead, the dean of American church history, links two phenomena to describe the reigning form of Protestantism in the second half of the nineteenth century. First, the social outlook was "too modern," that is, the life of the churches was accommodating complacently to the democratic faith of American destiny. Second, theology became increasingly irrelevant and anachronistic. Mead points out that these combined phenomena were hit by changes on two fronts. Urbanization, industrialization, immigration, economic crises, strikes, and populist politics were among the "perils" a contemporary commentator like Josiah Strong saw facing Americans. Along with social upheavals, Mead notes, went exacting challenges to traditional thinking, principally from Darwinianism, "higher" biblical criticism, and visionary utopianism. This confrontation, Mead concludes, led to a split in American Protestantism—a yet unresolved break between what historian Martin Marty calls the "private party" of fundamentalism and the "public party" of liberalism.[3] Living amid such challenges, many Americans were optimistic about the promise of prosperity. Thus was anxiety gilded with energetic hopefulness.

Like the work of historian Arthur M. Schlesinger, Sr., on whom he relies, Mead's analysis views religion primarily as a response to social and cultural conditions. We can see the dynamic, creative role of religion in this time more clearly by examining the life and work of two exemplary figures. Psychologist and philosopher William James developed his religious ethics as one cognizant of the period's intellectual challenges. Pastor and teacher Walter Rauschenbusch worked out his Social Gospel as one aware of the painful social changes of the day. Both men were dissatisfied with the divorce between thought and action that plagued their contemporaries. James attacked this problem more theoretically, Rauschenbusch more practically. Since religious concerns led both of them to ethics, we can see how ethics emerged as a lively way of being religious in the complacent culture of the Gilded Age.

Historian Bruce Kuklick has recently shown that midway through the nineteenth century, philosophers at Harvard served their community by defending Unitarian views against the rival faiths of Transcendentalism on the left and Calvinism on the right. But the new Darwinian science challenged all religious faiths, and Harvard philosophers began to investigate ways of reconciling the new science with religion. Darwin's *Origin of the Species* ran counter to the traditional Christian view of the Divine Creation of world and consequently questioned the kind of God in whom Christian—and others in a strongly Protestant culture—had conventionally believed.

Yet if the Bible and the theologies based on its revelations were no longer reliable as authoritative foundations for religious thought, philosophers concerned with religion still had several options. Josiah Royce investigated the problem of human knowledge and constructed a new argument for the Absolute. George Santayana hoped to salvage religion by linking it with poetry and aesthetics. William James relied on common human experience and developed a way to defend the proposition that, despite new challenges to traditional theism, people still ought to be moral and had a right to believe in God.[4] James spoke for many in the nineteenth century who became increasingly subjective in their approach to religion.

William James exemplifies what Donald H. Meyer has called "perhaps the last generation among English-speaking intellectuals able to believe that man was capable of understanding his universe, just as they were the first generation collectively to suspect that he never would."[5] Like many thinkers troubled by the "Victorian crisis of faith," James sought to preserve the essentials of religion by proposing a new basis for the kind of morality Christianity had traditionally and at its best supported. Thomas Carlyle in England and Albrecht Ritschl on the Continent, to name only two luminous contemporaries, were also finding the essence of religion in morality. "An ever-increasing emphasis on the ethical substance of religion was inevitable," Stow Persons observes, "as miracle and plenary inspiration lost their traditional authority."[6] Keenly aware of the crucial importance of metaphysical ideas and attuned to the way a world view sustains meaningful experience and supports constructive moral action, these late nineteenth-century thinkers were much concerned with ethics. If we broadly define the field of ethics as reflection on moral concerns, we can see that ethics was a way of being religious for intellectuals undergoing the Victorian crisis of faith. Because ideas and social patterns changed so quickly, moral behavior seemed the stronghold of traditional values and ethics the last arena for the interplay of religious beliefs.

James is exemplary among such thinkers, as his colleague George Herbert Palmer wrote:

> In him science and humanism were singularly combined. Learned as he was, he had none of the pedantry of the scholar. His books, besides illuminating their subjects, were creatures of character, and through them he became one of the chief spiritual forces of our time. . . . The universal admiration given him was ever mixed with love. From him men drew their ideals of human character and were grateful to him for being what he was.[7]

By his own confession, James was not a systematic thinker, yet the image of man in all his writings is remarkably coherent. This coherence can best be seen by tracing the development of James's "ethics of experience."

After an unusually free and in some ways frustrating childhood, William James became an "ethicist." Reading the French philosopher Renouvier, James brought himself out of the vitiating doldrums of a paternally protracted adolescence by recognizing that the first act of a free will is to declare its own freedom, an insight that helped him to begin his own life and work as a thinker. While his first real work was in physiology and especially psychology, James was all the time treating moral concerns. Although he produced many essays and addresses on moral topics, his first book—written at the age of forty-eight—was his massive *Principles of Psychology*. He wanted to develop a scientific form of introspection, to investigate individual consciousness in a scientifically supportable way. His own strenuous Puritanism surfaces occasionally in this text, as when he moves from an examination of cortical anatomy to an admonishment of moral habits. Some of the topics investigated psychologically in *The Principles* become crucial themes in James's ethics. Santayana was right about the importance of *The Principles*: all of James's thinking grew from the image of man he worked out as a psychologist.

Late in life, James labeled his way of thinking "radical empiricism." Unlike a priori rationalists, he was committed to experience as the basis of human knowledge. Yet unlike conventional empiricists who followed Hume in splitting truths of fact from truths of reason, James was committed to the wholeness of experience. His writing in *The Principles* on the importance of "fringes" of consciousness, and on the necessity of thinking of consciousness as a "stream," presages his radical brand of empiricism. Likewise, James's later "pluralistic" metaphysics—his view that reality is manifold, changing, and growing—is grounded in his psychology of the continuity of consciousness, especially in his desire to be true to both the "substantive" and the "transitive" stages of experience.

Similarly, James's "pragmatic" epistemology grows from his psychology. He argues that "truth" is not a property ideas have in themselves, apart from experience, but is instead something that "happens to" ideas in our experience. Ideas "become" true in life, as we attend to one thing rather than to something else, as we commit ourselves to one course of action or reflection rather than another. His chapters on "Attention" and "Will" set the stage for James's epistemological claim that knowing is an activity involving the whole person. Toward the end of his life, James wrote in *A Pluralistic Universe* that "we use what we are and have, to know; and what we know to be and have still more. Thus do philosophy and reality work in the same circle indefinitely."[8] Such pragmatism was James's way of being philosophically true to his psychological convictions.

Even during the generative period of *The Principles*, James sometimes addressed moral concerns more directly. In "The Dilemma of Determinism," he says, when facing the problem of evil, the "soft" determinist retreats into "gnosticism" (evil occurs for reasons we can never understand), and the "hard" determinist has to overcome his feelings of regret (evil is simply fate). James refused to disown the feeling of regret—how otherwise would we recognize evil?—or to defer quietly to the intellectual compensations of an Absolute Answerer (God has his own purposes; we grow through suffering; everything will work out in the end). Instead, James argued for the freedom of the will, and for a view of the world supporting it, since any other position entailed passivity or detachment from experience.

James's personal moral ideas—freedom, openness, spontaneity, individuality, commitment, work—are those which support the whole self in the struggle against evil. His social ethics are also rooted in his psychology. The ideals of democracy, the sacredness of individuals and their right to freedom and self-determination, grow from a sympathetic readiness to see life from the perspective of other whole persons. James's moral essays, such as "The Moral Philosopher and the Moral Life," often conclude with an argument for believing in the kind of God who supports, even needs, responsible free humane action: a finite God who depends on men to complete his creation. Conversely, James argues that such action is the measure of our "Will" or, better, our "right" to believe.

When James delivered the Gifford Lectures in Scotland, he broke with custom and traditional religious thought and examined "the varities of religious experience." There the psychologist was at work, cataloging the vagaries and excesses of religious lives. Particularly interested in the phenomenon of the "divided self," James finds more profundity in the conversion or "twice-born" religion of the "sick" soul than in the "once-born" strenuous moralism of the "healthy" soul. He describes his own sense of religion as a process of self-transcendence. By opening subliminal consciousness, a new selfhood is created, a selfhood in touch with a "MORE" available for real effects in human life through a shifting of one's "personal center of energy."

James describes his own "paltry overbelief" as the "crass" or "piecemeal" form of supernaturalism, as distinguished from the "refined" and rarified recourse to an ethereal Absolute sought by philosophers such as Royce. Certainly James was not so interested in theological construction as in pursuing a moral analysis of religion. His criteria for assessing the truth and value of religious phenomena are "immediate luminousness, philosophical reasonableness, and moral helpfulness." Conversion was of much interest to him because it made possible a demonstrably "saintly" form of behavior. Even when speaking directly to the topic, James's interest in religion was rooted in his psychology and was expressed predominantly in his concern for the ethics of individual experience.

As he elaborated the image of man first developed in *The Principles*, James was very much a philosopher—not in the current narrow professional sense, but in the sense of a man who thought deeply and hard about life. He was so thoroughly a man of thought, and so little a man of social action, that at least two writers have been at pains to point out the "warts" on his otherwise nobly remembered face.[9] But it seems unfair to score James for failing to develop programs that could put his ideas into practice. He was, after all, an individualist, and one sees the impress of his ideas and values on his own life clearly enough.[10] He obviously had little interest in, awareness of, or talent for social action. The relevant interpretive point here is that such a split between ethical reflection and social action broadly characterizes the religious life of the Gilded Age. James and his colleagues at Harvard created the "Golden Age" of American philosophy, but there were few overt connections between their reflections and the active side of religious ethics embodied in the Social Gospel. Indeed, this lively reform campaign suffered the converse problem. Even its most articulate proponent, Walter Rauschenbusch, toughened his thinking only when the movement was on the wane.

Granting the significant differences in their work—James the philosopher, Rauschenbusch the reformer—there are several important similarities in the substance of their ethics. James rejected absolute idealism and determinism because of their inadequate treatments of evil. Likewise, Rauschenbusch thought that most of the new theology tried to explain sin away in terms of the environment and that the old theology failed to recognize sin when actually confronted with it in society. Similarly, while the moral attitude of much philosophical spirituality was passive, James's religion actively encouraged moral involvement in life. Above all, James wanted a real engagement with life. As he put it in the conclusion of the *Varieties*:

> A bill of fare with one real raisin on it instead of the word "raisin," with one real egg instead of the word "egg," might be an inadequate meal, but it would at least be a commencement of reality. . . . I think, therefore, that however particular questions connected with our individual destinies may be answered, it is only by acknowledging them as genuine questions, and living in the sphere of thought which they open up, that we become profound. But to live thus is to be religious.[11]

Looking at the decorous worldliness of his time, Rauschenbusch found that "our industrial individualism neutralizes the social consciousness created by Christianity," and he came out, like James, for vital religion, urging both church and state to recognize that "together they serve what is greater than either: humanity. Their common aim is to transform humanity into the Kingdom of God."[12] Both James and Rauschenbusch wanted an ethics that would be effective in the fight against evil and, allied with such an ethics, a lively, dynamic, momentous kind of religion.

Writing about the erstwhile Unitarian Octavius Brooks Frothingham, Stow Persons makes a point that applies equally well to both James and Rauschenbusch:

> There was a profound sense of a deep gulf separating the modern age from the past. The historians of a later day were to attribute this to the industrial revolution. To contemporary thinkers like Frothingham [read: James and Rauschenbusch], however, the most persuasive indications of the unique character of the modern age were not industrial or material but moral, spiritual, and intellectual.[13]

Responding as they did to these cultural correlatives of industrialism, James and Rauschenbusch were important spokesmen for what Persons calls "the widespread tendency to reinterpret theological dogmas in moral terms."[14] But while James was pursuing this task by developing his ethics of individual experience, Rauschenbusch was as much if not more concerned with public problems. And while James worked out his psychology and philosophy in response to the challenges given to religion by the new science, Rauschenbusch propounded the Social Gospel in response to what he saw as the dehumanizing impact of rapid social change. James's books, essays, and talks were addressed to fellow philosophers, scientists, and cultured humanists. Rauschenbusch turned the message of the gospel against the churches and the powerful managers of social change.

The warm piety Rauschenbusch inherited from a long family line of Lutheran and German Baptist ministers broke down when he saw how many of his first parishioners, working-class German Baptists on the border of Hell's Kitchen in New York City, were "out of work, out of clothes, out of shoes, and out of hope."[15] The young pastor worked with his people, studied in Germany, and assumed a position on the faculty of Rochester Dvinity School. As a professor, he trained the consciences of many young ministers and wrote lively indictments of the complacent capitalist ethos. Since he is widely recognized as a chief spokesman of the movement, perhaps we can best understand the ethics of the Social Gospel by assessing the distance Rauschenbusch traveled between his two great works, *Christianity and the Social Crisis* and *A Theology for the Social Gospel*.

First published in 1907, several times reprinted, and selling eventually over 50,000 copies, *Christianity and the Social Crisis* was a challenging book. Its argument ran two ways: first, Rauschenbusch brought his view of the gospel to bear upon the moral problems of industrial, urban America; then, he turned the message of Christianity back to Christians. No individuals or institutions were exempt from the moral tangles of modernity. The book was primarily a sermon directed at his co-religionists. Summing up his analysis, Rauschenbusch wrote:

Primitive Christianity, while under the fresh impulse of Jesus, was filled with social forces. In its later history, the reconstructive capacities of Christianity were paralyzed by alien influences, but through the evolution of the Christian spirit in the Church it has now arrived at a stage in its development where it is fit and free for its largest social mission. At the same time Christian civilization has arrived at the great crisis of its history and is in the most urgent need of all moral power to overcome the wrongs which have throttled other nations and civilizations. The Church, too, has its own power and future at stake in the issues of social development. Thus the will of God revealed in Christ and in the highest manifestations of the religious spirit, the call of human duty, and the motives of self-protection, alike summon Christian men singly and collectively to put their hands to the plough and not to look back until public morality shall be at least as much Christianized as private morality now is.[16]

Given his pressing theological and historical analysis, it is disheartening in the chapter titled "What to Do," to read:

All that we as Christian men can do is to ease the struggle and hasten the victory of the right by giving faith and hope to those who are down, and quickening the sense of justice with those who are in power, so that they will not harden their hearts and hold Israel in bondage, but will "let the people go." But that spiritual contribution, intangible and imponderable though it may be, has a chemical power of immeasurable efficiency.[17]

Instead of attempting to change radically the structure of society, Rauschenbusch recommends redirecting current human relations toward higher ends: "The fundamental contribution of every man is the change of his own personality."[18] Enlightened youth will change the world when they come to power. Ministers ought to teach from the pulpit about "pressing questions of public morality."[19] The religious spirit should assert "the supremacy of life over property"[20] especially by aligning the church with the fraternal "communistic" interests of the rising working class. There must be an "apostolate of a new age" to "do the work of the sower" of the seeds of a new order,[21] for "the championship of social justice is almost the only way left open to a Christian nowadays to gain the crown of martyrdom."[22]

Although Rauschenbusch knew that "at best there is always but an approximation to a perfect social order" and that "the kingdom of God is always but coming," he was convinced that "every approximation to it is worth while."[23] Indeed, he sensed that "sometimes the hot hope surges up that perhaps the long and slow climb may be ending," for "if the twentieth century could do for us in the control of social forces what the nineteenth did for us in the control of natural forces, our grandchildren would live in a society that would be justified in regarding our present social life as semi-barbarous."[24] His belief that "the swiftness of evolution in our own country proves the immense latent perfectibility in human nature" enables him to conclude rhapsodically:

> Last May a miracle happened. At the beginning of the week the fruit trees bore brown and greenish buds. At the end of the week they were robed in bridal garments of blossom. But for weeks and months the sap had been rising and distending the cells and maturing the tissues which were half ready the fall before. The swift unfolding was the culmination of a long process. Perhaps these nineteen centuries of Christian influence have been a long preliminary stage of growth, and now the flower and fruit are almost here. If at this juncture we can rally sufficient religious faith and moral strength to snap the bonds of evil and turn the present unparalleled economic and intellectual resources of humanity to the harmonious development of a true social life, the generations yet unborn will mark this as that great day of the Lord for which all ages waited, and count us blessed for sharing in the apostolate that proclaimed it.[25]

So it appeared to the prophet in 1907.

But the swift eruption of the Great War made such hopefulness appear naive—made that time seem to be, as Henry James remarked, "the age of the mistake." Yet the disillusioning effects of the war revealed to Rauschenbusch a problem even more profound than the lists of casualties and the shocking accounts of destruction. Like the "lost generation" of imaginative writers, Rauschenbusch learned from the war that even the best critics of his time had failed to gauge the extent and power of evil. So, in 1917, he undertook to write *A Theology for the Social Gospel*, attempting to formulate the implications of these late disasters for the practice of Christian ethics.

The primary task, as Rauschenbusch saw it, was to readjust theology "so that it will furnish an adequate intellectual basis for the social gospel.[26] He continued to see the double nature of the task: "the social gospel needs a theology to make it effective; but theology needs the social gospel to vitalize it."[27] And since he knew, like William James, that "religion wants wholeness of life,"[28] Rauschenbusch sought to bring Christians of different traditions together. By reinterpreting his Baptist heritage in the light of events of the time, he wanted to reappropriate classic Christian symbols and doctrines:

> The social gospel is the old message of salvation, but enlarged and intensified. The individualistic gospel has taught us to see the sinfulness of every human heart and has inspired us with faith in the willingness and power of God to save every soul that comes to him. But it has not given us an adequate understanding of the sinfulness of the social order and its share in the sins of all individuals within it. It has not evoked faith in the will and power of God to redeem the permanent institutions of human society from their inherited guilt of oppression and extortion. Both our sense of sin and our faith in salvation have fallen short of the realities under its teaching. The social gospel seeks to bring men under repentance for their collective sins and to create a more sensitive and more modern conscience.[29]

Rather than repudiating the traditional emphasis on personal conversion, Rauschenbusch enlarges the idea of salvation to include society as well as the individual.

More than ever, Rauschenbusch was convinced that "our Christianity is most Christian when religion and ethics are viewed as inseparable elements in the same single-minded and whole-hearted life, in which the consciousness of God and the consciousness of humanity blend completely."[30] But his program was not a matter of arcane speculation. Since "religious experience, as William James has shown us, has many varieties, and some are distinctly higher than others,"[31] what Rauschenbusch hoped for was "a democratic change in theology on the basis of religious experience."[32] While he addressed many traditional doctrines and symbols in this way, to show that social gospel was "neither alien nor novel" but a repristination of basic Christianity, Rauschenbusch primarily tackled three clusters of symbols: the nature of sin and evil, the idea of God, and the atoning work of Christ.

Although "by our very nature we are involved in tragedy,"[33] Rauschenbusch recognized "it is possible to hold the orthodox doctrine on the devil and not recognize him when we meet him in a real estate office or at the stock exchange."[34] A new consciousness of sin comes when men sense the failure of their unspent energies or glimpse the ways they have "blocked . . . the essential aim of God himself."[35] And "the social gospel opens our eyes to the new ways in which religious men do all these things. It plunges us in a new baptism of repentance."[36] But instead of repeating traditional theology's emphasis on the original fall of man, which, he claimed was not important to the Hebrew prophets or to Jesus, Rauschenbusch said that Christians would do better by "concentrating their energies on the present and active sources of evil and leaving the question of the first origin of evil to God."[37] Looking at the present, Rauschenbusch affirmed the "remarkable unanimity" of theology's "ethical and social definition" of sin as "essentially selfishness."[38] But even as selfishness, "sin is not a private transaction between the sinner and God. Humanity always crowds the audience-room when God holds court."[39] Hence Rauschenbusch analyzed selfishness in the work of "the super-personal forces of evil."

All human institutions can fall prey to "the Kingdom of Evil": "our theological conception of sin is but fragmentary unless we see all men in their natural groups bound together in a solidarity of all times and all places, bearing the yoke of evil and suffering."[40] No one was exempt. In fact, "the higher the institution, the worse it is when it goes wrong. The most disasterous backsliding in history was the deterioration of the Church."[41] Rauschenbusch endorsed President Wilson's April 1917 address to Congress that "the Governments of Great States too may be super-personal powers of sin."[42] And "there is no doubt that these charges justly characterize the German government." But the prophet went further: "there is no doubt that they characterize all governments of past history with few exceptions, and that even the democratic governments of today are not able to show clean hands on these points."[43]

Rauschenbusch enforced his idea of the Kingdom of Evil by reappropriating an old and powerful symbol: "The ancient demonic conception and the modern social conviction may seem at first sight to be quite alien to each other. In fact, however, they are blood-kin."[44] Even in ancient Jewish times, "Satan first got his vitality as an international political concept,"[45] and, when early Christianity confronted the Roman Empire, "the belief in a Satanic kingdom of evil drew its concrete meaning and vitality from social and political realities. It was their religious interpretation."[46] Rauschenbusch applied the meaning of this reinterpreted symbol to his own day:

> The popular superstitious beliefs in demonic agencies have largely been drained off by education. The conception of Satan has paled. He has become a theological devil, and that is an attenuated and precarious mode of existence. At the same time belief in original sin is also waning. These two doctrines combined,—the hereditary racial unity of sin, and the supernatural power of evil behind all sinful human action,—created a solidaristic consciousness of sin and evil, which I think is necessary for the religious mind.[47]

Declaring "the salvation of the individual is, of course, an essential part of salvation,"[48] Rauschenbusch felt "it is time to overhaul our understanding of the kind of change we hope to produce by personal conversion and regeneration. . . . If sin is selfishness, salvation must be a change which turns a man from self to God and humanity."[49] William James would have agreed with Rauschenbusch that:

> It is faith to see God at work in the world and to claim a share in his job. Faith is an energetic act of the will, affirming our fellowship with God and man, declaring our solidarity with the Kingdom of God, and repudiating selfish isolation. . . . In the long run the only true way to gain moral insight, self-discipline, humility, love, and a consciousness of coherence and dependence, is to take our place among those who serve one another by useful labor. Parasitism blinds; work reveals.[50]

Reaching the theological conclusion that "the salvation of the composite personalities, like that of individuals, consists in coming under the law of Christ,"[51] Rauschenbusch spelled out the practical ethical requirements:

> The fundamental step of repentance and conversion for professions and organizations is to give up monopoly power and the incomes derived from legalized extortion, and to come under the law of service, content with a fair income for honest work. The corresponding step in the case of governments and political oligarchies, both in monarchies and in capitalistic semi-democracies, is to submit to real democracy. Therewith they step out of the Kingdom of Evil and into the Kingdom of God.[52]

Given his reinterpretation of sin, Rauschenbusch contended "the Church is the social factor in salvation"[53] but only—as, he notes, Josiah Royce had argued—if it embodies the revolutionary force of Christ.[54] Returning to his basic message, he declares "this conditional form of predicating the saving power and spiritual authority of the Church is only one more way of asserting that in anything which claims to be Christian, religion must have an immediate ethical nexus and effect."[55] Lest his Christian readers rest easy in the church, Rauschenbusch again spelled out his meaning: "The saving power of the Church does not rest on its institutional character, on its continuity, its ordination, its ministry, or its doctrine. It rests on the presence of the Kingdom of God within her."[56] Hence a modern social consciousness of sin and salvation requires a new vision of the Kingdom of God and a new understanding of God himself.

Rather than a naive dream of heaven on earth, the Kingdom of God was important for Rauschenbusch as an ideal image of a dynamic, social form of religion "in the public life of humanity."[57] Distinguishing his vision from that of an older, individualistic Christianity, he writes, "the saint of the future will need not only a theocentric mysticism which enables him to realize God, but an anthropocentric mysticism which enables him to realize his fellowmen in God."[58] Though many of his concerns were with practical morality, Rauschenbusch was theologian enough to know that his convictions about the social consciousness of sin and his commitment to the kingdom of God required a reimagination of the divine. In one of his most powerful passages, he sounds almost like Emerson in articulating an idea of God for the Social Gospel:

> God is not only the spiritual representative of humanity; he is identified with it. In him we live and move and have our being. In us he lives and moves, though his being transcends ours. He is the life and light in every man and the mystic bond that unites us all. He is the spiritual power behind and beneath all our aspirations and achievements. He works through humanity to realize his purposes, and our sins block and destroy the Reign of God in which he might fully reveal and realize himself. Therefore our sins against the least of our fellow-men in the last resort concern God. Therefore when we retard the progress of mankind, we retard the revelation of the glory of God. Our universe is not a despotic monarchy, with God above the starry canopy and ourselves down here; it is a spiritual commonwealth with God in the midst of us.[59]

Speaking with daring familiarity, Rauschenbusch claims "the worst thing that could happen to God would be to remain an autocrat while the world is moving toward democracy. He would be dethroned with the rest."[60] Showing his basic difference from William James, Rauschenbusch holds that "for one man who has forsaken religion through scientific doubt, ten have forsaken it in our time because it seemed the spiritual opponent of liberty and the working people."[61] Since he is looking at the social relevance—rather than the philosophical coherence—of the idea of God, he can say that "the Kingdom of God is the necessary background for the Christian idea of God. . . . a theological God who has no interest in the conquest of justice and fraternity is not a Christian. It is not enough for theology to eliminate this or that autocratic trait. Its God must join the social movement. The real God has been in it long ago."[62] Uniting theological insight with social concern, Rauschenbusch is moved almost to poetry:

> A God who strives within our striving, who kindles his flame in our intellect, sends the impact of his energy to make our will restless for righteousness, floods our sub-conscious mind with dreams and longings, and always urges the race on toward a higher combination of

freedom and solidarity,—that would be a God with whom democratic and religious men could hold converse as their chief fellow-worker, the source of their energies, the ground of their hopes.[63]

If sin is the negative expression of human solidarity, God is its positive foundation. "God is the common basis of all our life. Our human personalities may seem distinct, but their roots run down into the eternal life of God."[64]

Beyond his importance as the symbolic link between God and the social life of humanity, Jesus is important to Rauschenbusch as the initiator of the Kingdom of God. Reexamining the theological problems of the person and work of Christ brings Rauschenbusch to a reinterpretation of the doctrine of the Atonement which supplies the lynchpin of his entire ethical argument. He enumerates six public sins that combined to kill Jesus:

> Religious bigotry, the combination of graft and political power, the corruption of justice, the mob spirit, militarism, and class contempt,—every student of history will recognize that these sum up the constitutional forces in the Kingdom of Evil. Jesus bore these sins in no legal or artificial sense, but in their impact on his own body and soul. He had not contributed to them, as we have, and yet they were laid on him. They were not only the sins of Caiaphas, Pilate, or Judas, but the social sin of all mankind, to which all who have ever lived have contributed, and under which all who have ever lived have suffered.[65]

Accordingly, Rauschenbusch's new theory of the atonement "is not a legal theory of imputation, but a conception of spiritual solidarity, by which our own free and personal acts constitute us partakers of the guilt of others."[66] So too Rauschenbusch changes the conventional image of Jesus. His is no "gentle Jesus meek and mild," but one whose "head was up." Even on the cross, Jesus was "in command of the situation."[67] In reconceiving the Atonement in terms of the social nature of sin and evil, Rauschenbusch risks a novel conjecture about God:

> If we think of God in a human way, it seems as if the death of Jesus must have been a great experience for God. Pantheistic philosophy

represents God as coming to consciousness in the spiritual life of men and rising as our race rises. If we believe that he is immanent in the life of humanity and in a fellowship of love with us as our Father, it does not seem too daring to think that our little sorrows and sins might be great sorrows to him, and that our spiritual triumphs might be great joys. What, then, would it mean to God to be in the personality of Jesus and to go through his suffering and death with him? If the principle of forgiving love had not been in the heart of God before, this experience would fix it there. If he had ever thought and felt like the Jewish Jehovah, he would henceforth think and feel as the Father of Jesus Christ. If Christ was the divine Logos—God himself expressing himself—then the experience of the cross reacted directly on the mind of God.[68]

In *Christianity and the Social Crisis*, Jesus had been important as a prophet challenging the present-day church to undertake the work of social reconstruction. In *A Theology for the Social Gospel*, Rauschenbusch responds with theological imagination to the social nature of sin and evil; the work of Christ becomes more profound. If Jesus was a prophet, Rauschenbusch conjectures, he could have lived another thirty years. "There would have been an ample element of prophetic suffering without physical death. Death came by the wickedness of men. But taken in connection with his life, as the inevitable climax of his prophetic career, his death had an essential place in his work of establishing solidarity and reconciliation between God and man."[69] Thus Rauschenbusch's realistic attention to evil enables him to go beyond the liberal view of Jesus as prophet and moral exemplar in his early book and to reappropriate—in a new social way—the more traditional doctrines of the divine nature of the person of Christ and the atoning work of Christ as a reconciliation of God and man.

In turn, his reappropriation of traditional doctrines deepens Rauschenbusch's prophetic social ethics:

Thus the cross of Christ contributes to strengthen the power of prophetic religion, and therewith the redemptive forces of the Kingdom of God. Before the Reformation the prophet had only a precarious foothold within the Church and no right to live outside it. The rise of free religion and political democracy had given him a field and a task. The era of prophetic and democratic Christianity has just begun. This concerns the social gospel, for the social gospel is the voice of prophecy in modern life.[70]

If the devastation of the Great War and frenetic complacency of the "return to normalcy" of the 1920s, together with the deaths of its great leaders, spelled the end of the Social Gospel as a movement, Walter Rauschenbusch had nevertheless developed a theological ethic that could serve as a resource for future religious critics of American complacency—such as Martin Luther King, Jr.

James and Rauschenbusch—the philosopher and the reformer—worked creatively in a culture otherwise generally characterized by the sloppy fit between its ethos and its world view. Behind the thin screen of respectability was a cauldron of self-seeking and confused values, fired by social change and stoked by new ways of thinking. In addition to the Golden Age of philosophy at Harvard and the Social Gospel movement, there were other indicators of cultural creativity. Populist and Progressive politics, the temperance campaign, women's suffrage, Christian socialism, the trade union movement, literary realism, new theology, muckraking journalism—signs of the feeling that so much was possible when so much was wrong. Many of the symbols of late nineteenth-century America, whether progressive or conservative, tapped the emotional resources of evangelical Protestantism. Yet the liveliest cultural form of religion was no longer the social organization of the denominational institutions, but an ethic of experience and reform.

The changes to which Walter Rauschenbusch responded in writing *A Theology for the Social Gospel* shortly snuffed out the Social Gospel as an overt movement. But as theologian John C. Bennett has pointed out, "whatever may be true of the social gospel as a movement, there is no general return to a pre-social gospel individualism and privatism."[71] Professionalization narrowed the scope of American philosophy, but lively thinking about religion and morality continued outside the philosophic academy. In fact the ethics of both James and Rauschenbusch show that the past is prologue. Religious ethics continue to respond to the incongruity between the American behavior and the ultimate norms or sanctions of the moral life.

Each episode in the story of religion in American culture becomes a chapter out of which a new episode evolves. The period between the two world wars saw a lively reinvestigation, not so much of ethics per se, as of the fundamental religious beliefs that support and sustain Christian faith and morals. The reexamination was pursued most vigorously by Reinhold Niebuhr and most trenchantly by his brother H. Richard Niebuhr. These two theologians are often called "neo-orthodox," as if they were abandoning the liberal tradition in favor of simply restating old ideas. But we shall see that they are truly critical sons of the Social Gospel.

NOTES

1. Richard Hofstadter, *The Age of Reform: From Bryan to F. D. R.* (New York: Alfred A. Knopf, 1974), p. 60.

2. Clifford Geertz, *The Interpretation of Cultures* (New York: Basic Books, Inc., 1973), p. 89.

3. Sidney E. Mead, *The Lively Experiment: The Shaping of Christianity in America* (New York: Harper and Row, 1963), pp. 134-87. See also Martin E. Marty, *Righteous Empire: The Protestant Experience in America* (New York: Dial Press, 1970), pp. 133-220.

4. Bruce Kuklick, *The Rise of American Philosophy: Cambridge, Massachusetts, 1860-1930* (New Haven: Yale University Press, 1977).

5. D. H. Meyer, "American Intellectuals and the Victorian Crisis of Faith," in Daniel Walker Howe, ed., *Victorian America* (Philadelphia: University of Pennsylvania Press, 1976), p. 65.

6. Stow Persons, "Religion and Modernity, 1865-1914," in James Ward Smith and A. Leland Jamison, eds., *The Shaping of American Religion* (Princeton: Princeton University Press, 1961), p. 386.

7. Palmer, quoted in Kuklick, pp. 336-37.

8. William James, *A Pluralistic Universe* (New York: Longmans, Green, and Company, 1909), p. 330.

9. George R. Garrison and Edward H. Madden, "William James— Warts and All," *American Quarterly* 29, no. 2 (Summer 1977): 207-21.

10. See Gay Wilson Allen, *William James: A Biography* (New York: The Viking Press, 1967).

11. William James, *The Varieties of Religious Experience* (New York: Collier Books, Macmillan Publishing Company, Inc., 1961), p. 388.

12. Walter Rauschenbusch, *Christianity and the Social Crisis* (New York: Harper and Row, 1964), pp. 388, 380.

13. Persons, "Religion and Modernity," p. 381.

14. Ibid., p. 384.

15. Rauschenbusch, quoted in Ronald C. White, Jr., and C. Howard Hopkins, *The Social Gospel: Religion and Reform in Changing America* (Philadelphia: Temple University Press, 1976), p. 36.

16. Rauschenbusch, *Christianity*, p. 343.

17. Ibid., p. 411.

18. Ibid., p. 412.

19. Ibid.

20. Ibid., p. 413.

21. Ibid., p. 416.

22. Ibid., p. 418.

23. Ibid., p. 421.

24. Ibid.

25. Ibid., p. 422.

26. Walter Rauschenbusch, *A Theology for the Social Gospel* (Nashville: Abingdon Press, 1945), p. 1.

27. Ibid.

28. Ibid., p. 9.

29. Ibid., p. 5.

30. Ibid., p. 14.

31. Ibid., p. 19.

32. Ibid., p. 21.

33. Ibid., p. 32.

34. Ibid., p. 35.

35. Ibid., p. 37.

36. Ibid.

37. Ibid., p. 44.

38. Ibid., p. 47.

39. Ibid., p. 48.

40. Ibid., p. 81.

41. Ibid., p. 73.

42. Ibid., p. 74.

43. Ibid., p. 75.

44. Ibid., p. 87.

45. Ibid., p. 88.

46. Ibid., p. 89.
47. Ibid., p. 90.
48. Ibid., p. 95.
49. Ibid., p. 97.
50. Ibid., pp. 102, 103.
51. Ibid., p. 111.
52. Ibid., p. 117.
53. Ibid., p. 119.
54. Ibid., p. 128.
55. Ibid., p. 129.
56. Ibid.
57. Ibid., p. 145.
58. Ibid., p. 108.
59. Ibid., p. 49.
60. Ibid., p. 178.
61. Ibid.
62. Ibid.
63. Ibid., p. 179.
64. Ibid., p. 186.
65. Ibid., pp. 257-58.
66. Ibid., p. 259.
67. Ibid., p. 263.
68. Ibid., p. 264.
69. Ibid., p. 266.
70. Ibid., p. 279.
71. John C. Bennett, "The Social Gospel Today," in White and Hopkins, p. 293.

7

THE TWO NIEBUHRS: A MODERN THEOLOGICAL RENAISSANCE

After the First World War, Americans lived in a new world. Complex changes brought mixed reactions; there was no broadly accepted, easily recognizable way of characterizing the times. A term often used was "modern"—a chronological label suggesting novelty and revealing the lack of common cultural denominators. Several influences combined to create a situation in which theology was reborn as a vital cultural form of religion.

Spared the material destruction experienced by Europeans, Americans nevertheless were deeply disillusioned by the war. Though many were bravely ingenuous during the "roaring twenties," the war's psychic challenges could not be ignored. During the Great Depression many questioned if the business of America was really business, as President Coolidge had preached, and economic recovery was painfully slow. The rise of fascism and European remilitarization made it plain that the "war to end all wars" had failed and might better have been called the First World War. When World War II broke out, dreams of American isolation were again interrupted. The siege mentality of the Cold War, together with actual combat in Korea, made wars and rumors of wars a continuing source of anxiety.

At the same time, the social "perils" of the Gilded Age and the intellectual challenges of the "Victorian crisis of faith" continued to disturb the comfort of the churchly and to reduce their numbers. "Modern" people seemed to ignore the message and the relevance of Christianity. The previous generation had debated what sort of morality Christians ought to have. Now the pressing question was what, if anything, Christianity had to contribute to the task of coping with the moral complexities of modernity. Such a question was almost beyond the limits of moral argument and ethical reflection. The only satisfactory answers to such "meta-ethical" concerns would have to be theological. The bases of faith and morals needed reexamination, and such investigation is one of the principal tasks of theology.

At first glance, theology might appear outmoded—dry speculation on recondite matters like infant damnation or the degrees of eternal punishment for predestined sins. Yet some modern theologians sloughed off arcane images, and their vocation experienced a brilliant renaissance. Like the work of such giants as Augustine, Aquinas, Luther, Calvin, Schleiermacher, and Edwards, the task of modern theology is, as Schubert Ogden notes, "the attempt, within the context of the given witness of the Christian community, to try to think critically about the meaning and truth of that witness, and in doing so to make use of whatever conceptual resources are necessary to do that adequately." The careers of Reinhold and H. Richard Niebuhr show that, as Ogden reiterates, "the job Christian theology has to do, very simply, is to ask the question of the meaning and truth of the Christian witness of faith in our world."[1]

Yet in a brief and characteristically blunt "intellectual autobiography," Reinhold Niebuhr said, "I cannot and do not claim to be a theologian. . . . I have never been very competent in the nice points of pure theology; and I must confess I have not been sufficiently interested . . . to acquire the competence."[2] If theology is esoteric and abstract, neither Niebuhr was very theological. Both spoke to real people in understandable language about how to cope with the unavoidable problems of life. They were not "academic" or "foundational" theologians, nor were they philosophers of religion. Instead of questioning the philosophical foundations or the intellectual legitimacy of religion, the Niebuhrs sought ways to understand the implications of Christian faith in their world. Without sacrificing its integrity, their goal was to formulate the basic Christian message for modern people. In their books, theology regained its cultural role as a vital way of being religious.

After his collegiate and theological education, Reinhold Niebuhr, like his father, entered the parish ministry. For thirteen years, the young pastor of the Evangelical Synod of North America ministered to the working people of Henry Ford's emergent "motor city." The efficiency of Detroit's factory system was a model for the industrial world, but its human costs haunted Niebuhr for the rest of his life. His first book asked *Does Civilization Need Religion?* Niebuhr's prodigious theological output can be interpreted as his attempt to articulate a satisfactory affirmative response. In 1928, he joined the faculty of Union Theological Seminary, where he spent his life sharpening the conscience of young ministers, speaking on college campuses, and writing for national journals.

The contours of Reinhold Niebuhr's career match those of Walter Rauschenbusch's life. Like Rauschenbusch at Rochester, Niebuhr's seminary position was a platform for prophecy. He too brought to American society a judgment of its ideals. Yet his vision was substantially different from that of his Social Gospel precursor. Ever attentive to irony and paradox, Niebuhr's view of life was darker, and he often criticized the Social Gospel and what he called "liberal Christianity" for its naivete. Indeed the cultural impact of Niebuhr's *Moral Man and Immoral Society*, written in 1932, was similar to Rauschenbusch's *Christianity and the Social Crisis*. But Niebuhr's sober moral analysis upset readers who had not been alert to developments during the twenty-five-year period between the two books. As a contemporary recalled, Niebuhr's book seemed "especially to those of the older generation, to be the outpouring of a cynical and perverse spirit, very far removed from the benevolent and sanguine serenity which was held to be the hallmark of a truly Christian mind." Such readers found "their dearest assumptions concerning man's perfectibility, his kinship with the divine, his natural goodness . . . demolished with ruthless iconoclasm."[3]

Moral Man and Immoral Society was so upsetting because Niebuhr argued, as the title implies, that although individuals can sometimes act morally, social groups find it nearly impossible to put the interests of others before their own. As small groups merged into larger ones, Niebuhr saw human relations becoming increasingly ruthless. Since economic, political, and military power grow with the self-seeking of all collectives, a morality based on individual goodness is superfluous piety. Niebuhr unsparingly scored modern educators and religious idealists for failing to understand the brutal behavior of human collectives and the power of self-interest in all intergroup relations. Echoing such Founding Fathers as John Adams and James Madison, Niebuhr concluded that relations between groups must be seen as predominantly political rather than ethical.

Once attention was focused on political methods, Niebuhr proposed two criteria for assessing their worth. First, do they do justice to man's moral and rational capacities? Second, do they take adequate account of those human limitations that are so undeniably active in collective life? This sort of questioning exposed the poverty of the preceding generation's social morality. Yet Niebuhr's constructive suggestions for achieving and preserving social justice were even more troubling than his basic interpretation of the extent of egoism in human relations.

Like many intellectuals in the 1930s, Niebuhr believed that the Marxists had correctly analyzed the social problems of modern industrial life. Yet he felt that their advocacy of violence endorsed the wrong means for fighting injustice; he could not share their hope for a new age of tranquil equality following the anticipated revolution of the proletariat. Selfishness would not disappear, and in his view it was a romantic illusion to look for such a dramatic change in social life. He found Communist messianism a form of idolatry and a most dangerous one. On the other hand, neither did Niebuhr find a solution in parliamentary socialism, which too often capitulated to its opposition and relied too much on the personal character of its leaders. In fact, moral values could be preserved in social relations, he thought, only by doing justice to the insights of both the religious moralists and the political realists. Niebuhr placed his hope, if anywhere, in the coercive power of movements of non-violent resistance.

This early book was important primarily for the realistic way it raised moral questions. Finding adequate answers required more work. The moral resources of religion could be unlocked, Niebuhr felt, only by a fresh, realistic appraisal of human nature. The pressing needs of modernity were ill served by ideals of personal charity and dreams of social perfectibility. Answers came a decade later, with the publication of his Gifford Lectures, *The Nature and Destiny of Man*. Prompted by the urgent need for realistic social and political action, Niebuhr turned more directly toward theology to examine the bases of Christian faith and morals. Always a prophet, and preaching whenever he wrote, Niebuhr had—for the sake of ethics—become a theologian.

Because, in his view, life in the modern world required it, Niebuhr's goal was to resuscitate the Christian view of man. He thought people were inclined to forget that it is man's nature to be a problem to himself. As Herman Melville knew, man is both a child of nature and also a spirit who stands outside of nature, life, himself, his reason, and the world. Hence man has the capacity for self-transcendence, but he is also tied to nature and its limits. Man is neither animal nor God. Because modern life tempts people toward one side or the other of this essential paradox, Niebuhr sought to reintroduce them to themselves. He had to show the resources of a true image of man in order to indicate the sources of modern confusion. Then the Christian view of man could serve as a corrective sufficient for modern needs.

According to Niebuhr, in the Christian view, man is by nature a unity of body and soul. Christianity sees God as the Creator of a good world; man's finiteness of body and spirit is not a dilemma to be escaped, but is intrinsically good. Instead of denying that he is a limited creature, man should be understood from the standpoint of God. As a creature with a body *and* a spirit, man often feels out of place in the world. This sense of homelessness to which religions universally minister testifies to the necessity of seeing man in terms of God. In addition, Christianity values man's individuality. The sense of individuality man finds in self-transcendence is not an illusion; indeed, it rests on God's disclosure of his own personality and will in the individuality of Christ. Yet Christianity also asserts that man is a sinner, not by accident but by the rebellion of will against

God. However difficult it may be to admit or to express, man is a sinner and confirms this fact every day in history. In addition, for the Christian, man lives both within and—by virtue of his capacity for self-transcendence—outside of history.

These elements of the Christian view of man made it the answer for modern man. But Niebuhr knew it was not so simple. Other images competed with the Christian view for man's allegiance. The chief opponent, historically, was the classical view of man. Here man is understood from the standpoint of the uniqueness of his rationality. Man's reason is seen as his link to the divine, his way of escaping what the Greeks considered the illusion of individuality. At present, according to the classical view, man is a frustrating duality of mind and body. The task and glory of the mind is to liberate man's quasi-divine spirit from the evils of bodily existence. Given the brevity of life, the certainty of mortality, and the fact that only a few are truly wise, the classical view of man is essentially pessimistic—even ultimately tragic—in that man's creativity comes at the price of disturbing the eternal divine order of things.

In Western history, argues Niebuhr, a new view of man emerged when a compound of elements from the classical and Christian traditions was mixed with elements uniquely modern. From the classical tradition came the concept that man should be understood primarily from the standpoint of either the uniqueness of his reason or his involvement with nature. Modern idealists developed the classical rationalist emphasis on man's reason. Modern naturalists saw nature as a harmless realm of order and peace, and modern romantics, who saw nature as the source of man's creative vitality, continued to view man in terms of his affinity with nature. From the Christian tradition, bolstered by the rise of the bourgeoisie, came the conviction that every man has value as an individual. And from the technological triumphs of modernity came the view that man is essentially good—the belief that man can have an "easy conscience" since there is no such thing as original sin or radical evil. If man is seen primarily as rational, evil appears to result from his dependence on nature, and freedom is won through more and better reasoning. If man is seen primarily as a natural being, evil appears to be rooted in the misuse of reason, and freedom is found in a return to nature. This modern amalgam is what Niebuhr wanted to dissolve.

Reinhold Niebuhr was, in the best sense of the word, an apologetic theologian. He saw that the basic problem of Christianity in the modern world is not that it is unbelievable; rather, because of certain inadequate and inconsistent views of man, it is alleged to be irrelevant. Before demonstrating the adequacy of Christianity, Niebuhr had to establish its relevance. Its relevance, he was convinced, was in the way its view of man clarified the problems of modern life.

Hence, to validate his arguments, he appeals, as did James, to his audience's sense of personal experience rather than to biblical norms or to any other external authority. This method makes *The Nature and Destiny of Man*, as a reviewer remarked in 1941, a "treatise in empirical theology."[4] If modern man examines the facts of his own experience, Niebuhr wagers, he will find the Christian view more adequate than the "easy conscience" alternatives. Christianity affirms the individual's sense of being a creature of both nature and spirit. It supports one's feeling that individuality is irreducibly valuable. And it explains the unavoidable presence of evil in human life. Throughout the book—indeed throughout his life—Niebuhr is saying, "Look at your own life. Doesn't the Christian view finally make sense of what would otherwise remain a puzzling frustration?" Many of his contemporaries were convinced.

Niebuhr has two basic ways of validating his Christian interpretation of man. First, he argues that the general revelation given to every individual, and the special revelation given in social history, demonstrate the power of the Christian view to illumine the heights of man's self-transcendence, the extent of his finite dependence on the contingent necessities of nature, and the evil in his heart and in his relations with others. Second, Niebuhr argues that some such revelation is the only way to ground *any* interpretation of human experience. The full meaning of an experience can be grasped only by referring to something beyond the experience itself. This may seem to involve a logical circle, but, argues Niebuhr, "the fact is that all human knowledge is so involved." Experience either is so amorphous as to have no discernible meaning, or it has some reality beyond the experience which provides a context for its interpretation. And if the reality beyond experience is made known to us then "the principle of interpretation must be something more than merely the general principles of knowledge which illumine a particular experience. The principle of interpretation must be a 'revelation.' "[5] Thus Niebuhr argues both *from* and *to* experience as the basis of the Christian view of man.

As a Christian, Niebuhr is not convinced that human experience sufficiently reveals it own meanings, for "the God whom we meet as 'The Other' at the final limit of our consciousness, is not fully known to us except as specific revelations of His character augment this general experience of being confronted from beyond ourselves."[6] He explains this claim by another appeal to experience. For if a person does not pay attention to the special revelation of the Bible, his "easy conscience" will falsify the fact that something beyond itself is required to make sense of its experience. The "easy conscience" will merely appeal to "the court of social approval," or to the person's own "best self." Then, regardless of any initial uneasiness, "the final verdict always is, 'I know nothing against myself' and the conclusion drawn from this verdict must be and is, 'I am thereby justified.' " But, says Niebuhr, "this conclusion is at variance with the actual facts of the human situation, for there is no level of moral achievement upon which man can have or actually has an easy conscience."[7]

Such telling insight into the conversations an individual has with his conscience enable Niebuhr to develop a "negative proof for the Biblical faith." The biblical view is presented as the necessary corrective to the modern failure "to appreciate either the total stature of freedom in man or the complexity of the problem of evil in him."[8] So Niebuhr appeals to revelation as the ground of the truth of the Christian view of man, and he affirms the adequacy and relevancy of that view in the facts of human experience. He is then prepared to say just what the Christian view of man entails, not in opposition to competing views, but in itself.

Niebuhr sees three basic ideas in the Christian doctrine of man. It is perhaps characteristic of him to deal with the first two (man as image of God and as creature) in a single chapter and to take four chapters to discuss the third (man as sinner). Summing up what it means to hold that man is made in the image of God, he writes:

> By virtue of his capacity for self-transcendence he can look beyond himself sufficiently to know that a projection of himself is not God. This does not mean that he will not commit idolatry and make God in his own image. Man is constantly tempted to the sin of idolatry and constantly succumbs to it because in contemplating the power and dignity of his freedom he forgets the degree of his limitations.[9]

An individual's "creatureliness" is closely related to his status as an image of God. God created man as finite. Finitude is something man should, trusting God, affirm. But that rarely happens, and Niebuhr points out "that Jesus' injunction, 'Therefore I say unto you be not anxious' contains the whole genius of the Biblical view of the relation of finiteness to sin in man. It is not his finiteness, dependence and weakness but his anxiety about it which tempts him to sin."[10] These first two basic ideas in the Christian view of man are critical because they help Niebuhr explain the causes of the anxiety that is the precondition of man's sin. Niebuhr is at his prophetic best in analyzing sin, and it is here that his view of self-transcendence finally becomes clear.

If people trusted in God from the outset, sin would not occur. But this has never happened. Because individuals do not immediately trust in God, the paradox of their finiteness and freedom inevitably generates anxiety. If people trusted in God, this paradox would be a spring for creativity. But, in their unbelief, anxiety tempts them either toward pride (an unfounded faith in one's power, knowledge, virtue, or spirituality) or toward sensuality (an escape from freedom by identifying only with one's natural finiteness). Niebuhr finds that many Roman Catholics and liberal Protestants overemphasize the individual's freedom when analyzing sin, and that many fundamentalists overemphasize the individual's natural depravity. Niebuhr's own view—which he calls the "biblical" one—avoids the shortcomings of these other views and is more consonant with actual experience, because it preserves the sense of both nature and spirit in people's lives. By distinguishing between man's essentially good nature and the existential problem of not conforming to that nature, Niebuhr maintains both a sense of sin's inevitability and the idea of one's responsibility for it. He removes "original righteousness" from a mythic past and locates it—as a sense of "law" and "love" contending within the divided self—in man's memory. Analyzing anxiety and sin brings Niebuhr to explain how the crucial experience of self-transcendence occurs.

As Niebuhr's analogue of conversion, self-transcendence depends upon a Pauline sense of the divided self. On the one hand, the self looks out upon the world from the perspective of its own values and necessities. On the other hand, the self looks at its own actions in the world and is disquieted by its own undue claims. In intense self-searching, these two selves come together to consciousness, revealing that *"The 'I,' which from the perspective of self-transcendence, regards the sinful self not as self but as 'sin,' is the same 'I' which from the perspective of sinful action regards the transcendent possibilities of the self not as self but as 'law.' It is the same self; but these changing perspectives are obviously significant"* (Niebuhr's emphasis).[11] These changing perspectives enable the self to place its confidence in God. Thereby anxiety is relieved, and the self is liberated from its bondage to itself and freed for creative action in the world. One could slip into pride in one's experience of self-transcendence. But insofar as one continues to trust in God and his acceptance and support of one's confidence, faith completes revelation. Such contrition and appropriation of divine mercy are the fulfillment of man's life.[12]

In the second volume Niebuhr argues that God's revelation in Christ shows the meaning and the limits of history. Self-transcendence frees man toward mutual love. True mutual love is possible only from the standpoint of sacrificial love; only because of God's previous forgiveness and acceptance can sinful man place his trust in God and become free to love others unselfishly. Since God's love is not limited by the history in which it is expressed, it discloses the limitations of all actual mutual love. Seen in relation to history, the cross of Christ becomes a symbol that refutes both those who would find meaning only within history and those who want to transcend their involvement with history. The love of Christ is thus ethically normative, and the highest perfection for man is to achieve a unity that is "a harmony of love in which the self relates in its freedom to other selves in their freedom under the will of God."[13]

In a sense, the two volumes of *The Nature and Destiny of Man* reintegrate the Puritan synthesis of personal conversion and social responsibility. But, unlike the Puritans, Niebuhr implies that man may progressively—albeit not quite fully—complete himself in history. When Niebuhr turns from human nature to human destiny, he shows, for all his scoring of the naivete of liberal Christianity, that he is perhaps best characterized as a critical son of the Social Gospel. The unity he foresees at the end of time was prefigured in the beginning; the tensions and paradoxes of history are interim problems, though of long duration. This direction of thought presumes a nonhistorical definition of what man really is.

Niebuhr tends to view the Atonement as an interim strategy for an interim problem, rather than as an essential part of God's life. He claims that the Atonement is crucial, but one may ask whether Niebuhr's analysis of human destiny really needs the Christ. Indeed, Jesus and the cross are moral influences, and revelation clarifies something in a person's self-understanding rather than effecting something genuinely new. Against the Christocentrism and Christian exclusivism of continental contemporaries like Emil Brunner and Karl Barth, Reinhold Niebuhr looks considerably more liberal than "neo-orthodox." His analysis of human nature may have been more soberly realistic than Rauschenbusch's, but his hope was the same—the old, renewed Puritan desire for purity in the public realm to match the spiritual cleansing of inward conversion.

If his vision of the "last things" was similar to Rauschenbusch, Niebuhr was in another way heir to the individualism of William James. Niebuhr's early distinction between the morality of individuals and the immorality of social groups had a lasting effect. As he explains it, the crucial experience of self-transcendence seems to occur in a "vertical" vacuum existing between the self and God, and only secondarily to have "horizontal" implications and consequences in one's interpersonal and social actions. Except for *The Self and the Dramas of History* (where the "dialogues" of the self with itself, with God, and with the neighbor are still perhaps too neatly delineated), history seems for Reinhold Niebuhr simply to be the horizontal plane on which an individual interacts with others rather than an essential dimension of one's own life.

Perhaps Niebuhr's commitment to realistic social and political action, like his belief in the transcendent mercy and judgment of God, was so deeply a part of himself that it framed the context— rather than supplying the specific issues—for his thinking. Certainly he was critical of what he called Harvard orthodoxy—the acceptance by his secular friends of the Christian diagnosis of the human situation but not the Christian remedy. He was always an effective preacher of the Christian view of man and a vigorous prophet in turning its insights toward illumining the complexities of modern life. The fact that despite his disavowels, he so often adopted the theological mode in his analysis says as much about his times as it does about the man himself. Religion in the "modern" period required a searching reexamination of traditional ideas of God and man. No one in America surpassed Reinhold Niebuhr's vigor in this task. His only equal had a voice less widely heard, but a mind more penetrating. Whatever Reinhold Niebuhr lacked in theological acumen was compensated by the trenchant brilliance of the work of his brother, H. Richard Niebuhr.

Helmut Richard was the youngest of the Niebuhr children. He trained for the ministry in his father's and brother's steps. In addition to gaining a theological education in America and Germany, Richard served as pastor, professor, and college president before accepting the position at Yale Divinity where he trained a generation of young ministers and wrote most of his important books. Even in his teaching, he was reticent about his personal experiences. It is fair, then, to concentrate on the development of his thinking made public in his writings.

H. Richard Niebuhr's first book, *The Social Sources of Denominationalism*, written in 1929, introduces his lifelong concern with the role of religion in social history. Building on the work of Ernst Troeltsch, Niebuhr investigated religious institutions with the cold eye of a social scientist. Like Reinhold, Richard's early work was influenced by Marxism. He attacked the class-based economic order baptized by the churches. He wrote vividly—his memorable first sentence is "Christendom has often achieved apparent success by ignoring the precepts of its founder." And his purposes were explicit:

> The problem of the world is the problem of a synthesis of culture. . . . And every civilization which has possessed itself by possessing such a synthesis has received it from its religion. . . . Compared with [the] ethical syntheses of its cultural forebears the modern world is atomic, confused, divided. . . . Civilization, which has always in the past depended upon its religious faith for the discovery and assertion of its values, cannot produce out of itself the devotion to a common spiritual end which will unite rather than divide it. . . . But the dilemma of the Western world lies in the fact that . . . the only religion available seems incapable of establishing, even within its own structure, the desired harmony.
>
> Hence there is abroad the cry for a new religion. . . . But new religions do not rise at the call of need; if they do appear they come in organic, evolutionary continuity with the religions of the past which they absorb and reaffirm. . . . However great may be the distance between the creed and the practice of Christendom, yet this civilization in its whole structure, from fundamental, unconscious ideas about personality and progress to the character of its economic and political life, has been conditioned by its religion. It can no more deny this fundamental factor in its cultural heredity than it can gainsay its biological sources. It is the product of its faith and by its faith it stands or falls.[14]

It is not surprising that this careful social scientist involved himself in efforts for the renewal of Christianity. In 1935, for example, with Wilhelm Pauck and Francis P. Miller, Niebuhr criticized the church's unconscious connections with nationalism, capitalism, and humanism. Their book was titled *The Church Against the World*.

Although he was aware of "the problem of a constructive Protestantism"—a tradition of critical protest that supplied scant resources for forming a new society—he continued his analysis of religion in American history in *The Kingdom of God in America*

(1937). Building upon his earlier work, but altering its Marxist thrust, Niebuhr began to probe for the dynamic currents of American Protestantism. He was convinced that religion should be understood as a living movement, rather than as a congeries of static institutions. He saw the relation between God and the world as a moving dialectic of worship and work. And he believed firmly that "apart from God the whole thing is meaningless."[15]

Operating with these convictions, Niebuhr found the dominant idea of the kingdom of God played with different emphases at different times in America. The Puritans interpreted the kingdom in terms of the sovereignty of God, the revivalists in terms of the reign of Christ, and the liberal reformers in terms of the kingdom on earth. As a confessing participant within the movement whose life he was interpreting, Niebuhr had moved from sociological analysis to a historiography of meaning. Sounding like his hero Jonathan Edwards, in a famous sentence Niebuhr castigated the naive optimism of liberal Protestantism: "A God without wrath brought men without sin into a kingdom without judgment through the ministrations of a Christ without a cross."[16] Critic that he was, Niebuhr still recognized that "the same institutionalism which represents the death of an old movement can be, as history amply demonstrates, the pregnant source of new aggression." And he was hopeful that the spiritual restlessness of the Social Gospel and other reform movements "manifested increasing interest in the great doctrines and traditions of the Christian past, as though they were aware that power had been lost because the heritage had been forgotten, or that there was no way toward the coming kingdom save the way taken by a sovereign God through the reign of Jesus Christ."[17] As a historian, he saw that theology could help the church live and move in the right direction.

As he pursued answers to the questions raised in these early analytical books, H. Richard Niebuhr became increasingly theological. *The Kingdom of God in America*, looking beyond *The Social Sources of Denominationalism* for the dynamic currents of American Protestantism, locates a central theme but also raises the question of how God acts in history. Such an inquiry may be beyond the bounds of the study of history, and one of the principal tasks of theology is to answer such "meta-historical" questions. Niebuhr's compact book of 1941, *The Meaning of Revelation*, did just this, and its publication showed that, without losing his interest in social history, Niebuhr had become a thoroughgoing theologian.

Niebuhr set forth his basic convictions about revelation in a characteristically straightforward manner. First, self-defense is the most prevalent source of error in all thinking. Stated positively, this means people can be justified only by grace, not by their own works or ideas. Second, the great source of evil in life is the absolutizing of the relative. Stated positively, this means that only God is sovereign, and that no human endeavors should be accorded the ultimacy that belongs to God alone. Third, Christianity is permanent *metanoia* or revolution. By extension, this means that beyond human finiteness there is an eternal life. And Niebuhr acknowledged his intellectual debts to the critical social analysis of Ernst Troeltsch and to the constructive theology of Karl Barth.

Then he spoke directly to the main problem of historical and religious relativism. If religions are like other social and cultural phenomena conditioned by history, how can a particular religion claim to bear eternal truths? How can a modern man be a theologian? Niebuhr came quickly to "the sum of the matter":

> Christian theology must begin today with revelation because it knows that men cannot think about God save as historic, communal beings and save as believers. It must ask what revelation means for Christians rather than what it ought to mean for all men, everywhere and at all times. And it can pursue its inquiry only by recalling the story of Christian life and by analyzing what Christians see from their limited point of view in history and faith.[18]

Proceeding with this specific task, Niebuhr argues that Christians must attend to the "reasons of the heart," since "revelation means for us that part of our inner history which illuminates the rest of it and which is itself intelligible."[19] Believers must examine the illuminating passages of their lived history and then seek corroboration or accept criticism from how they perceive God acting in external history. Listening to God speaking in their inner history reveals a pattern of dramatic unity which illumines past, present, and future.

In addition to judging the inner story of revelation by reference to external events of social history, Niebuhr had another, more theological method of evaluating the reasons of the heart. He argued that the change of the self that is the life of Christianity can only ensue from the revelation of God as a "Thou" who knows us. Authentic religion cannot be sustained by ideas about God, or by church institutions, or even by the example of Jesus. Outer history is not enough; inner history is required. An actual revelation of God's unity, power, and goodness, says Niebuhr, is not a possession but an event. Such an event calls into question those religious phenomena—ideas, institutions, values, even images of Jesus—that appear from an external perspective to be what Christianity is all about. Hence Niebuhr concludes that "this conversion and permanent revolution of our human religion through Jesus Christ is what we mean by revelation."[20]

Rather than proceeding in a conventionally philosophical or conceptual manner, Niebuhr argues appropriately for his position by confessing and articulating what he has learned about the transvaluation of selves and values in the event of revelation. Without sacrificing his tough-minded philosophical acumen, Niebuhr's method is appropriate to his understanding of the meaning of revelation. Many of his contemporaries found him legitimating a promising way for modern, historically conscious Christians to speak from faith about God and man. But the sticky question raised by the very success of Niebuhr's analysis of revelation is how the church, as the community faithful to the revelation of God, is to be related to the wider world. Niebuhr addressed this problem in his important and popular book, *Christ and Culture*.

Observing that reconciling the two poles of Christ and culture is the enduring problem of Christianity, Niebuhr again in this book of 1951 made his own convictions explicit: "Christ as living Lord is answering this question . . . in a fashion which transcends the wisdom of all his interpreters yet employs their partial insights and their necessary conflicts."[21] To find his answer as a theologian, Niebuhr used his powers of observation as a historian and social scientist to develop a typology of relations between the church and the world. On the one hand, there is an ongoing tension between two extreme positions—some Christians like Tertullian and Tolstoy see nothing of real value in human culture and other Christians like Abelard and Ritschl tend to see their own cultures as natural embodiments of the true faith. On the other hand, between the extremes of rejecting and accommodating culture, lie three intermediary positions. Some Christians like Clement and St. Thomas see Christ as essentially above yet involved in human culture. These believers seek a synthesis of Christianity and civilization. Other Christians like St. Paul and Luther see Christ and culture locked in paradox. These dualistic believers live in the world against the world. Still other Christians like F. D. Maurice and Niebuhr himself see Christ as the transformer of culture. Whichever position one takes—and Niebuhr notes the virtues and deficiencies of each—every believer confronts a basic dilemma. There is no escaping a decision, no "neutral" stance in relation to religion and civilization. Yet each believer's faith, like all human knowledge and action, is only relative in status. No human believer has an absolute perspective.

In 1948, Niebuhr wrote appreciatively about "the gift of the Catholic vision."[22] Perhaps one of his goals in *Christ and Culture*, written while Western civilization was attempting to recover from the Second World War, was to create an ecumenical, even universalistic, forum for religious concerns. In his "concluding unscientific postcript," he points out that whatever stance one takes, "in faith in the faithfulness of God we count on being corrected, forgiven, complemented, by the company of the faithful and by many others to whom he is faithful though they reject him."[23] Believers must make decisions about Christianity and civilization; the crucial thing is "to make our decisions in faith," which "is to make them in view of the fact that the world of culture—man's achievements—exists within the world of grace—God's Kingdom."[24] Evidently "the world of grace" was now in Niebuhr's mind including not only the church but also "many others to whom he is faithful though they reject him." This was a long step. Niebuhr's next book showed that he was ready to take it.

The publication in 1960 of lectures given in 1957—together with several earlier essays—under the title *Radical Monotheism and Western Culture* represents another stage in Niebuhr's theological development. In this book he attempts to work out the concluding implications of *Christ and Culture*. At the outset, he notes that "when I reflect on the present human situation it is the problem of faith that presents itself to me as of the greatest importance; and faith is to be distinguished from religion. We express it in our religion, to be sure; but also in all of our social decisions, actions, and institutions."[25] What Niebuhr now wants to understand is "a fundamental personal attitude which, whether we call it *faith* or give it some other name, is apparently universal and general enough to be widely recognized. This is the attitude and action of confidence in, and fidelity to certain realities as the sources of value and the objects of loyalty."[26] The neo-orthodox label so often appended to the Niebuhrs does not stick. Richard Niebuhr's analysis of faith now sounds much more like the open, mediating religiousness of Paul Tillich than the exclusivist Christianity of Karl Barth.

Examining the grounds of faith, Niebuhr again develops a typology. If one has confidence in and fidelity toward the One God, one's faith may be called "radical monotheism." If one has confidence in and loyalty toward a number of loosely related centers of value—home, family, career, possessions, church, nation—one's faith may be valled a modern form of "polytheism." Niebuhr contends, however, that "the chief rival to monotheism" in modern times "is henotheism or that social faith which makes a finite society, whether cultural or religious, the object of trust as well as of loyalty and which tends to subvert even officially monotheistic institutions, such as churches."[27]

Given such a wide-ranging definition of faith, Niebuhr sees a dual task for theology: to reason in faith and to criticize the faith in which one reasons. As he pursues this task, it is not surprising that Niebuhr sees radical monotheism—as Jonathan Edwards saw the nature of true virtue—as the only form of faith whose center of value is the principle of being itself. All other faiths are of less than ultimate value. Perhaps Niebuhr was disquieted by the revival of religion and the high figures of church attendance that pollsters gathered in the 1950s. In any event, he sought to demonstrate how often organized religion loses touch with the One God and becomes another form of henotheism. Christians have a tendency to place their confidence in and be loyal to the church itself, or to Jesus, instead of the God he pointed to and disclosed. However rarely tried, radical monotheism would certainly be a form of faith to transform culture. Here one sees Niebuhr developing a theology that could criticize and renew the social forms of faith he had always analyzed so adeptly.

A single question remained. Given Niebuhr's analysis of religion in history and his theological treatment of revelation and radical monotheism, how should a faithful Christian act in modern society? H. Richard Niebuhr died in 1962, but his lectures on ethics, published posthumously as *The Responsible Self*, speak to this point. Examining the meaning of responsibility, Niebuhr again develops a typology. One may see the individual primarily as a maker who asks the question "What is my goal, ideal, or telos?" Or one may see the individual primarily as a citizen who asks "What is the law and what is the first law of my life?" Or one may see a person primarily as an interacting responder to life who asks "What is going on?" The image of man as responder suits modernity well and is also, Niebuhr argues, full of moral possibilities.

Summarizing the ethics of these images of man, Niebuhr concludes:

> If we use value terms then the differences among the three approaches may be indicated by the terms, the *good*, the *right*, and the *fitting*; for teleology [man the maker] is concerned always with the highest good to which it subordinates the right; consistent deontology [man the citizen] is concerned with the right, no matter what may happen to our goods; but for the ethics of responsibility the *fitting* action, the one that fits into a total interaction as response and as anticipation of further response, is alone conducive to the good and alone is right.[28]

Richard Niebuhr has not enriched theological discourse by coining the term *cathekontic* to describe the ethics of responsibility. But he did define "the idea or pattern of responsibility" as "the idea of an agent's action as response to an action upon him in accordance with his interpretation of the latter action and with his expectation of response to his response; and all of this is in a continuing community of agents."[29] Responsibility is always social, for man interacts in a community of responders. And man as responder acts in history, considering both the past (interpreting the act to which he responds) and the future (anticipating a response to his own action). Niebuhr proposed that "the idea of the moral life as the responsible life in this sense not only has affinities with much modern thinking but also offers us, I believe, a key—not *the* key—to the understanding of that Biblical ethos which represents the historic norm of the Christian life."[30]

One whose faith takes the form of radical monotheism will find responsibility in "absolute dependence" upon God as his or her center of value. If one places confidence in and gives loyalty to the God upon whom alone one can absolutely depend, one can with Niebuhr affirm: "God is acting in all actions upon you. So respond to all actions upon you as to respond to his action."[31] Since Christ is our (but we cannot say only) symbol of universality, the believer whose faith has the form of radical monotheism knows Christ as the paradigm *of*, and the redeemer *to*, responsibility. Since Jesus saw cosmic generosity in natural and social events and acted in a way that looked forward to an infinite response, he is an example or paradigm for the moral life. And since Niebuhr believes that "the ultimate power does manifest itself as the Father of Jesus Christ through his resurrection from death," he also affirms Christ as the redeemer *to* responsible being who inaugurates and maintains the movement of Christians "toward their end and all endings as those who, knowing defeats, do not believe in defeat."[32] Niebuhr makes these final affirmations with conviction, but also with humility, as things "Christians cannot easily say."[33]

Building as it does on *The Meaning of Revelation* and *Radical Monotheism*, *The Responsible Self* demonstrates that one final product of Niebuhr's lifework is a new vision of Christian ethics. Despite his criticism of the Social Gospel, this abiding and, at least chronologically, ultimate concern with ethics may suggest that he, too, is best seen as a critical figure in the liberal Protestant tradition. But his trenchant theological examination of the bases of Christian faith and morals was not, I think, guided so completely by ethical concerns as was the work of a Walter Rauschenbusch. H. Richard Niebuhr's purpose seems more truly to fit the classical definition of theology as faith seeking understanding (*fides quarens intellectum*). Like other great theologians in the Christian tradition, he was wagering that such understanding would, in turn, enrich faith. As was appropriate for a man with such deep interests in the social and historical dimensions of life, the development of H. Richard Niebuhr's theology may be seen as leading toward the renewal of the church as the community of those who are faithful to the One God.

H. Richard Niebuhr examined the idea of God and the sense of human sociality that reigned as assumptions in Reinhold Niebuhr's analysis of the nature and destiny of man. It would be tempting to compare Reinhold as prophet to H. Richard as priest. But the difference in the styles and substance of their theologies is best shown by observing that Reinhold was characteristically a preacher, Richard a teacher. Reinhold worked out his theology as he brought his basic ideas about man to bear on current problems. Richard's theology—like the social faith he studied—was a dynamic movement, each book's answers raising larger questions for his next project. Perhaps more stirring to read, Reinhold was more successful in moving his secular contemporaries to consider the merits of the Christian view of man. Yet Richard's more careful work may be the richer resource for present and future religious thinking. Contemporary ethicist James Gustafson notes precisely why H. Richard Niebuhr should be remembered as "the theologian of the Christian life":

> Theology, he often said, is reflection on the action and nature of God; ethics is reflection on the response of man to the action and nature of God. One can see from this definition of Christian ethics that the philosopher of the Christian life had to become its theologian in order to develop a systematic Christian ethics, for the moral

life of the Christian community is *response to God*, the Creator, the Governor, and the Redeemer.[34]

Together, the two Niebuhrs' examination of the bases of Christian faith and morals is both vigorous and trenchant. Their work shows well how theology became a vital form of religion in modern culture.

Yet modernization proceeded with a vengeance in America following the Second World War, and the sense of a common audience to whom the Niebuhrs spoke rapidly disintegrated. The increasing "privatization" of religion and the growing "pluralization of social life worlds" led to new cultural forms of religion in American life.

NOTES

1. Proposed initially as a "thesis for discussion," the implications of this definition of theology and its task may be found elaborated in Schubert M. Ogden, "What is Theology?" *The Journal of Religion* 52, no. 1 (January 1972): 22-40.

2. Reinhold Niebuhr, "Intellectual Autobiography," in *Reinhold Niebuhr: His Religious, Social, and Political Thought*, ed. by Charles Kegley and Robert W. Bretall (New York: Macmillan Company, 1956), p. 3.

3. English theologian Alan Richardson, as quoted in Nathan A. Scott, Jr., *Reinhold Niebuhr* (Minneapolis: University of Minnesota Press, 1963), p. 15.

4. Calhoun, "Review," *The Journal of Religion* 21, no. 3 (October 1941): 473.

5. Reinhold Niebuhr, *The Nature and Destiny of Man, A Christian Interpretation. Volume I: Human Nature. Volume II: Human Destiny* (New York: Charles Scribner's Sons, 1941, 1964) 1:129-30.

6. Ibid., 1: 130.

7. Ibid., 1:130-31.

8. Ibid., 1: 131.

9. Ibid., 1: 166.

10. Ibid., 1: 168.

11. Ibid., 1: 278-79.

12. Ibid., 2: 56-57.

13. Ibid., 2: 95.

14. H. Richard Niebuhr, *The Social Sources of Denominationalism* (New York: The World Publishing Company, 1929, 1957), pp. 266-69.

15. H. Richard Niebuhr, *The Kingdom of God in America* (New York: Harper and Row, 1937, 1959), p. xvi.

16. Ibid., p. 193.

17. Ibid., p. 198.

18. H. Richard Niebuhr, *The Meaning of Revelation* (New York: The Macmillan Company, 1941, 1960), pp. 30-31.

19. Ibid., p. 68.

20. Ibid., p. 139.

21. H. Richard Niebuhr, *Christ and Culture* (New York: Harper and Row, 1951, 1956), p. 2.

22. H. Richard Niebuhr, "The Gift of the Catholic Vision," *Theology Today* 4, no. 4 (January 1948): 507-21.

23. Niebuhr, *Christ and Culture*, pp. 255-56.

24. Ibid., p. 256.

25. H. Richard Niebuhr, *Radical Monotheism and Western Culture, with Supplementary Essays* (New York: Harper and Row, 1960), p. 11.

26. Ibid., p. 16.

27. Ibid., p. 11.

28. H. Richard Niebuhr, *The Responsible Self: An Essay in Christian Moral Philosophy* (New York: Harper and Row, 1963), pp. 60-61.

29. Ibid., p. 65.

30. Ibid.

31. Ibid., p. 126.

32. Ibid. p. 177.

33. Ibid., p. 176.

34. James M. Gustafson, "Introduction," in H. R. Niebuhr, *Responsible Self*, p. 40. Gustafson's emphasis.

8

MODERNIZATION AND ITS DISCONTENTS

As "the first new nation" America was already "modern" in some important ways in its beginnings, states sociologist Seymour Martin Lipset.[1] Historian Richard D. Brown has traced the modernizing transformation of American life from 1600 to 1865.[2] But American life was not thoroughly, unalterably modern—in a substantive, distinctive way—until World War II. Military, industrial, and economic developments of the Second World War accelerated America's drive toward modernization, and the political, social, and cultural consequences of involvement in the war steered the course for future American life. Social scientists have defined "modernization" variously.[3] The cultural import of this complex process becomes clear when we investigate modernity, in Peter Berger's words, "as the institutional concomitants of technologically induced economic growth."[4] Several important concepts involved in the idea of modernization suggest how "the growth and diffusion of a set of institutions rooted in the transformation of the economy by means of technology"[5] created new role for religion in American life.

Social phenomena like modernization have both objective and subjective dimensions. An objective fact like a factory entails a host of subjective facts in the inner lives of its investors, managers, workers, and the consumers of its products. Together these objective and subjective facts make up a particular "social life-world." Following the phenomenological direction of Alfred Schutz, and relying upon his own work with Thomas Luckmann on "the sociology of knowledge," Peter Berger contends that "all social reality has an essential component of consciousness."[6] Because a number of individuals inhabit a particular social life-world, we may speak of the various meanings or "reality definitions" they share. Reality definitions need not be fully articulated in a conceptual way. Indeed, most of our meanings are pretheoretical clusters of symbols, values, and ideas. The constellations of consciousness associated with modernization have interesting implications for religion.

Technological production is a primary force of modernization, and its overt processes rebound upon the people it involves. In a modern factory, as Berger says, "the work process has a machine-like functionality so that the actions of the individual worker are tied in as an intrinsic part of a machine process."[7] An engineer who designs a machine may be creative; a person who operates the same machine all day does his job by becoming machine like or mechanistic. If the parts one produces are identically reproducible, so are the operators of the machines that make them. Rather than an expression of the worker's individuality, each task is important only as one part of the process. "Mechanisticity" and "reproducibility" go together in the worker's consciousness as they do in the design of an assembly line. The worker's task constitutes only one step in the overall process; his job—like the product he makes—is easily and precisely measurable.

Men and machines are components of production. Individual linkings of men and machines are parts of the process as a whole. The components and their sequences are interdependent; thus the means (the particular worker's task) and ends (the finished product) are neatly separable. The worker may feel little relation to the end product, and even less to the aims of management and rewards of ownership. There is an implicit abstraction about tasks that fit together like cogs on gearwheels. These aspects of the work process mean that the consciousness of those involved—whether workers, managers, investors, or consumers—in technological production has a "background" of "componentiality." Tasks may be altered and rearranged to improve the process as a whole; an attitude of continual tinkering is widespread in modern society. Institutions and social processes are adjusted and "tuned-up," often without regard for the individuals whose work constitutes the reproducible, mechanistic components of the process as a whole.

The upshot of technological production, as anyone who has worked on a factory line knows, is "the segregation of work from private life."[8] This is a good example of how increasing involvement with technology exacerbates tensions inherent in any complex society. When technology is pervasive and habitual, people may attribute to many of their social relations the kind of anonymity they experience at work. A double consciousness develops—people seeing themselves as individuals and also as faceless units in a production process or technological crowd. Alienation is widespread and characterizes consciousness in general. Individuality is suppressed in public and is free only in increasingly private realms of experience. Such a "cleavage in the emotional economy of the individual . . . produces anxiety" and calls for increasing "emotional management" as a form of psychic protection.[9] At the same time, the "bigger and better" orientation of technological production is internalized as a desire for maximizing one's "off the job" pursuits. Since so many things are going on at the same time, one feels like a component in a number of complex, interrelated processes. A frustrating feeling of "multi-relationality" may ensue. Individuals may consign responsibility for "the big picture" to the industrial, economic, military, and political managers who may control the social fates.

Perhaps no one is subject to all of the themes here associated with technology. Yet in most advanced societies, everyday life is widely bombarded with technological products and processes and the themes of consciousness they generate and sustain. Many of these themes contribute to what Berger calls "an overarching symbolic universe peculiar to modernity."[10] When the objective and subjective dimensions of social life are so powerfully redirected, forms of religion also will change. Because religion is only indirectly related to technological production, we can best see the role of religion in the modernization of American life by looking at the concurrent processes or carry-over effects of technology.

The idea of modernization illumines important cultural relations between apparently diverse religious events. Technology provides a thematic background for the bureaucratization that reshaped major religious institutions. The modern city's pluralization of social life-worlds gave broader cultural power to black religion. The rational temper of technology and bureaucracy heightened the crisis of religious plausibility that resulted in "the death of God." No one of these events "caused" the others, but certainly they fit together in the general picture of modernization.

Technology has been linked with bureaucracy as a primary carrier of modernity. The same rationality and efficiency that modernize production processes also shape various groups and their relations in technological societies. Bureaucratic social structures are objective facts with powerful subjective consequences. As institutions become more increasingly bureaucratic, so does the consciousness of the individuals whose lives they regulate and order. Yet if technology and bureaucracy often move in tandem, neither is fully dependent on the other. The government of ancient Rome, for example, was bureaucratic, but its primary means of production were not technological.

In modern societies, however, when the two processes reinforce each other, their full force is felt. Spurred by technology, modern bureaucracy seems almost to have a life of its own. Its way of organizing social interaction and its impact on consciousness soon extends from the factory into politics and into nearly every other aspect of life—including religion. Ironically, it is in the realm of religion, where each individual's innermost experiences are of paramount importance, that bureaucracy may best reveal the nature of its power.

Some of the major religious groups in America—Methodists, Presbyterians, Episcopalians, and Roman Catholics—have traditionally had hierarchical structures of power and authority exercising guidance and some control over their local congregations or parishes. Such groups anticipated the rational ordering of procedures and personnel that characterizes modern bureaucracy. One would expect these groups to be open to the ideas that officials are evaluated by criteria of competence rather than personality, that adequate coverage of problems is assured through established channels of referral and redress, and that proper procedures exist for delegating authority and ensuring just and orderly relations between individuals within the particular institution. Hence one is not surprised to find these denominations accommodating well to the bureaucratic tendencies of modern technological society. A better test case for assessing the spreading power of bureaucracy would be found in the Baptist tradition, which has taken pride in the freedom and autonomy of its local congregations from any hierarchical authority or external control.

In 1907 the Northern Baptist Convention (now called the American Baptist Churches, U.S.A.) was formed, with the goal of coordinating and regulating the efforts of several national evangelical and missionary societies. This was a radical step. Along with the "soul competence" of individual believers, Baptists have traditionally affirmed the sole spiritual authority of local congregations. As the work of the convention grew, it gained increasing legitimacy, largely because of its financial and administrative efficiency. The power of the national organization expanded, but its authority was based solely on its ability to raise money and solve problems, rather than on theology or spiritual experience. Paul Harrison argues persuasively that this incongruity between power and authority coincides with a belief held by many modern Baptists:

> The holy spirit works only at the level of the local communion; seldom, if ever, does the Spirit move through the efforts of the state or national boards. Thus a dichotomy is established between the associational groups and the local congregations. An essential difference is declared with respect to the nature of the two groups. The result is a tendency toward the total secularization of the associational agencies, but, on the other hand, an idealization of the spiritual potential of the local communions.[11]

The national and regional agencies of the convention provide important services, but American Baptists have not worked out a theological rationale for the authority of those who direct such work. Hence their national leaders have tended to be either charismatic figures or pragmatic executives. Naturally there has been considerable tension between these two types, and Harrison's "social case study" makes (for sociology) lively reading.

The presence of an influential hierarchy, as well as the absence of rules and traditions to govern its actions and authorize its status, means that this religious organization is sustained by pragmatic adjustments of means to goals and by the efforts of executives to preserve their programs. As Harrison observes, "the net effect is that the Baptist denomination, so proud of its heritage of social freedom and concern, is no less conservative and cautious than the highly rationalized ecclesiastical organizations."[12] In fact, many Baptists no longer comprehend their bureaucracy. Most of the denomination's active members work at only one level—national, state, regional, or local—and concentrate on only one or two of the total group's many concerns. The organization is characterized by pluralistic loyalties whose authority is merely bureaucratic; hence various agencies and programs compete for the attention, energy, and funding of local congregations.

As a believer in the tradition he criticizes, Harrison notes sympathetically that "the Baptists may have been wise when they removed the bishops from their places; but when they also eliminated the ecclesiastical authority of their own associations the bishops returned in business suits to direct affairs from behind the curtain of the center stage."[13] The problem is not limited to the churches. Indeed, as Harrision observes, "every voluntary and non-authoritarian association in America—trade unions, service clubs, patriotic and veteran's groups, quasi-religious groups, and business associations—become involved in the problem of the authority and power of their leadership."[14] The dilemma grows from the kind of denominational institutions the churches became in America. Yet Harrison warns that "no group can function without leadership, and it has been argued that when leaders are divested of authority they will necessarily seek and gain power in order to meet their responsibilities; the power they acquire may exceed that which ordinarily accrues to leaders in non-totalitarian, hierarchical institutions."[15]

Some of the Baptists' most distinctive doctrines have blinded them to characteristic features of their own organizations. Their original purposes were contrary to the beliefs and values of modernity. The goal of the convention was to convert individuals and to transform social structures, yet the organization itself has accomodated extensively to the procedures of modern bureaucracy. Bureaucracy's orderly, efficient, fairhanded advantages are hard for the members of a voluntary association to deny. But Baptists have not adjusted their doctrines to bring thinking into line with practice. The Baptist example suggests that modernity jeopardizes the connections between religious beliefs and their social expressions. Bureaucracy has been accompanied by the pluralization of social life-worlds, and this has hastened a general crisis in religious plausibility.

Technology and bureaucracy, along with urbanization and mass communications, have created many "worlds" for modern individuals. In traditional societies—or, as we have seen, in the vision of American Puritans—all of life's activities and meanings are integrated into a single world of experience. The unifying order of a traditional culture is expressed in its religion, which symbolizes how this world's coherence mirrors or replicates the order of the cosmos itself. When the forces of modernity began to dissociate the world of work from other aspects of life, the authority of religious symbols ceased to be unquestioned. As technology and bureaucracy reinforce each other, public and private life become less coherently related. Eventually what a person does for a living merely pays for—but does not necessarily otherwise determine—his life-style. Public and private aspects of experience may become different worlds. Perhaps an individual only endures the one for the sake of his "real" life in the other.

Awareness of the disjunction between the public and private spheres of one's life may breed anxious quests for certainty in one direction or the other. In addition, one has to deal with the different kinds of people compacted into a modern city, suburb, or industrial town. And the dazzling barrage of images and experiences purveyed by mass communications fragments and multiplies life-worlds within both public and private spheres. One's true identity and "right" social location become goals to be sought, rather than facts given at birth. Identity becomes the project—rather than a characteristic—of one's life. Playing a word association game, given identity, a traditional person might reply character or fate, whereas a modern probably would say crisis.

Although it posed many challenges for the psychology of individual religious experience, the pluralization of social life-worlds combined positively with other modernizing influences to broaden the general awareness and enhance the social power of black religion in America. While the religious history of black people in America is rich and complex, in recent times the fragmentation and growing diversity of experience within the dominant white culture provided a new chance for black people to move toward liberation. Even now, freedom is far from fully achieved, but it is interesting to note how modernization strengthened the cultural role of black religion in America.

Starting with Franklin Roosevelt's New Deal programs and continuing with other programs following the Second World War, the federal government assumed many of the economic and social services that were previously the responsibility of voluntary associations and private citizens. As this happened, the government became increasingly bureaucratic and—in theory at least—dealt with its "clients" more anonymously and gave them a more generalized expectation of justice. This meant that one could appeal to the government for redress of social injustice or other grievances suffered because, for example, one was black. Much progress toward racial equality was made in this way through legislation and the courts. Various laws, executive actions, and court decisions were made possible, indeed given cultural authority, by the rhetoric of black leaders who appealed to the values and manipulated the religious symbols of the sacred canopy that was disintegrating for many whites. Bureaucratization gave blacks the chance to appeal neutrally for their unprejudiced rights as citizens. And the pluralization of social life-worlds gave their appeal an opportunity to be delivered with religious power.

To work effectively in such a cultural situation, a black leader would have to be a syncretist. In addition to appealing to white

American symbols and values, he or she would have to provide a realistic focus for the hopes of black Americans. Martin Luther King, Jr., was such a leader. It is not surprising that such a scholarly authority on black religion as Joseph R. Washington, Jr., criticized King's "mixed salad bowl" thinking as a "hodge-podge" of Mahatma Gandhi, Jesus, and Baptist preaching, claiming that King's program was not Christian theology at all. Why was King's message so culturally powerful for both blacks and whites?

King did not base his appeals on the honor of the dominant white majority. As a moral value of great force in a static, hierarchical society, honor was giving way to the modern notion of dignity as the inherent value of the individual in a changing society.[16] Since dignity inheres in each individual, rather than belonging to the members of one caste as opposed to another, it could be affirmed both by modernized whites and by oppressed blacks.

In his last full-length book *Where Do We Go From Here: Chaos or Community?*, King spoke repeatedly of dignity, skillfully moving this modern point with the aid of traditional religious symbols. In 1967, he saw the internal resources of the black man:

> The Negro will only be truly free when he reaches down to the inner depths of his own being and signs with the pen and ink of assertive selfhood his own emancipation proclamation. With a spirit straining toward true self-esteem, the Negro must boldly throw off the manacles of self-abnegation and say to himself and the world: "I am somebody. I am a person. I am a man with dignity and honor. I have a rich and noble history, however painful and exploited that history has been. I am black *and* comely." This self-affirmation is the black man's need made compelling by the white man's crimes against him. This is positive and necessary power for black people.[17]

Even while contending that each man must be dealt with "as a person sacred in himself," King's tone was sometimes calmly analytical: "So long as the Negro or any other member of a minority group is treated as a means to an end, the image of God is abused in him and consequently and proportionately lost by those who inflict the abuse."[18] At other times, his language was passionately conclusive: "In the final analysis the white man cannot ignore the Negro's problem, because he is part of the Negro and the Negro is part of him. The Negro's agony diminishes the white man, and the Negro's salvation enlarges the white man."[19] The variety of his rhetoric enabled him to speak, indeed to preach, effectively to audiences divided by custom and history.

As a participant in the movement whose story he was interpreting, King knew the effects of modernity:

> Every man lives in two realms, the internal and external. The internal is that realm of spiritual ends expressed in art, literature, morals and religion. The external is that complex of devices, techniques, mechanisms, and instrumentalities by means of which we live. Our problem today is that we have allowed the internal to become lost in the external. We have allowed the means by which we live to outdistance the ends for which we live.[20]

King heard a religious answer in the "Hindu-Moslem-Christian-Jewish-Buddhist belief" that "love is the key that unlocks the door which leads to ultimate reality."[21] Yet he was realistic enough to know that "what is needed is a realization that power without love is reckless and abusive and that love without power is sentimental and anemic. Power at its best is love implementing the demands of justice. Justice at its best is love correcting everything that stands against love."[22] Modernity and its media of communication gave King several audiences. The appropriateness of his rhetoric to his cultural situation made him an effective preacher of the message articulated earlier by Walter Rauschenbusch and Reinhold Niebuhr.

Several years before his tragic death, King knew that his movement was no longer riding the high tide of the early 1960s. The nervousness he sometimes betrays in modifying or rejecting the "Black Power" slogan shows that he was troubled by the waning cultural power of his commitment to nonviolence. In the late 1960s the cultural spotlight shifted to leaders like Stokely Carmichael who spoke directly for "Black Power" as "the politics of liberation of America."[23] But the respect given to Dr. King and the cultural power of his syncretistic message are signs that the disintegration of a sacred canopy can sometimes be a very healthy thing for religion. Other ethnic and "new" religions appeared; the heretofore dominant canopy was definitely in trouble, and a remarkable group of theologians was joyfully singing its last rites.

In the 1960s modernization proceeded amid growing signs of discontent. As bureaucracy rationalized the turmoil of an individual's social relations and ordered the awesome otherness of mass society, technology demystified the natural order. As human ingenuity and power grow, technology and bureaucracy sometimes inspire their own sense of magic. Theologians are sensitive to such changes, especially insofar as the accompanying pluralization of social life-worlds intensifies the problems for religion. As Berger summarizes:

> Through most of empirically available human history, religion has played a vital role in providing the overarching canopy of symbols for the meaningful integration of society. The various meanings, values and beliefs operative in a society were ultimately "held together" in a comprehensive interpretation of reality that related human life to the cosmos as a whole. Indeed, from a sociological and social-psychological point of view, religion can be defined as a cognitive and normative structure that makes it possible for man to feel "at home" in the universe. This age-old function of religion is seriously threatened by pluralization. Different sectors of social life now come to be governed by widely discrepant meanings and meaning systems. Not only does it become increasingly difficult for religious traditions, and for the institutions that embody these, to integrate the plurality of social life-worlds in one overarching and comprehensive world view, but even more basically, the plausibility of religious definitions of reality is threatened from within, that is, within the subjective consciousness of the individual.[24]

Many people find such a crisis of religious plausibility frightening and hence seek renewals of old certainties. Yet some intellectuals in the 1960s discovered in the crisis an experience of liberation from what they saw as tired theological ideas, outworn religious images, and restrictive moral practices. They did not reject the culture that spawned the crisis, or try to transform modernity or accommodate the basic truths of religion to the current cultural trends. These intellectuals made a more radical move: they embraced the secularity of modern life and found criticizing religion a new way of being religious.

Among the most daring of the radical theologians, professors William Hamilton and Thomas Altizer proclaimed the death of God as a public event in the modern world. This did not mean simply that people needed new ways of thinking about God or required new images for expressing His reality—it meant that the being known as God had actually died. Together with God's death came the birth of new human beings, autonomous in their actions and knowledge and in full control of their own destiny. The historical Jesus, not the spiritual Christ, was taken as an example of an action-oriented life of service to one's neighbors—or when the situation demanded it, as a revolutionary. Other religious entities or theological categories were dispensed with as irrelevant to a secular age.

Beyond their power to exhilarate radicals or shock the complacent, such affirmations obviously expressed a real crisis of plausibility in religion. These men were not external observers; they lived the crisis out in their teaching and writing. Their most poignant statements concern the status of "the death of God theologian" himself. So long as their task was to criticize the unquestioned assumptions of orthodox belief, or to propose new interpretations of traditional ideas and new applications of basic values, the radical theologians had a religious audience. Nor could other theologians ignore the radical theologians' illustration of the problematic status of God-language in modern thought. They were important as critics.

But when the radical theologians tried to formulate their positive ideas, they experienced what H. Richard Niebuhr earlier identified as "the problem of a constructive Protestantism." No doubt people have too long anthropomorphized their images of God and need to be reminded of that fact. But if God actually died, what more was there for a theologian to say? Again, without God, why should modern people pay more attention to the man Jesus than to any other exemplary moral figure? Indeed, without God, Jesus might appear to be a lunatic. But the radical theologians were not primarily debating with other professionals. They were speaking from their experience of modernity to other people who felt the disparity between modernity and traditional religion.

Feature stories in national magazines indicated that the audience of radical theology was broad indeed. While the crisis of religious plausibility troubled theologians and the leaders of religous institutions, its force was also felt in peoples' lives as a subjective counterpart to the unremitting pressures of technology, bureaucracy, and pluralization. Though necessarily brief as a theological movement, "the death of God" remained an important cultural symbol. But the critique of religion was a short-lived way of being religious.

Radical theology's shocking negations about God were matched by what proved to be naive faith in the autonomous capacities of man "come of age." Riots in several major cities indicated that America's racial problems were far from over. The war in Vietnam could be neither won nor stopped. The youth rebellion, the Watergate crisis, the ecological movement, women's liberation, and economic recession coupled with inflation demonstrated that coping with modernization required more critical distance than one could find in the affirmations of secularity made by the radical theologians. Then too, a rash of new and renewing religious movements suggested that modern man was not so enduringly secular as his radical champions had claimed. Given the concurrent, cumulative effects of technology, bureaucracy, pluralization, and the crisis of religious plausibility, a new way of being religious in America came from one of the few remaining sources of vitality—the spirit within.

NOTES

1. Seymour Martin Lipset, *The First New Nation: The United States in Historical and Comparative Perspective* (New York: Basic Books, Inc., 1963).

2. Richard D. Brown, *Modernization: The Transformation of American Life, 1600-1865* (New York: Hill and Wang, 1976).

3. Compare David Apter, *Some Conceptual Approaches to the Study of Modernization* (Englewood Cliffs: Prentice-Hall, 1968), and *The Politics of Modernization* (Chicago: University of Chicago Press, 1963); J. A. Armstrong, "Development Theory: Taking the Historical Cure," *Studies of*

Comparative Communism 7 (Spring/Summer 1974); Mehmet Beqiraj, *Peasantry in Revolution* (Ithaca: Cornell University Press, 1966); Cyril E. Black, *The Dynamics of Modernization* (New York: Harper and Row, 1966); David R. Cameron, "Toward a Theory of Political Mobilization," *Journal of Politics* 36, no. 1 (February 1974); S. N. Eisenstadt, *Modernization, Protest and Change* (Engelwood Cliffs: Prentice-Hall, 1966), and *Tradition, Change, and Modernity* (New York: Wiley, 1973); Clifford Geertz, ed., *Old Societies and New States* (New York: Free Press of Glencoe, 1963); Joseph R. Gusfield, "Tradition and Modernity: Misplaced Polarities in the Study of Social Change," *American Journal of Sociology* 72, no. 4 (January 1967); Alex Inkeles and David Smith, *Becoming Modern* (Cambridge: Harvard University Press, 1974); Daniel Lerner, *The Passing of Traditional Society* (Glencoe, Ill.: Free Press, 1958); Marion Levy, Jr., *Modernization and the Structure of Societies* (Princeton: Princeton University Press, 1966), and *Modernization: Latecomers and Survivors* (New York: Basic Books, 1972); Alasdair MacIntyre, "A Mistake about Causality in Social Science," in Peter Laslett and W. G. Runciman, eds., *Philosophy, Politics and Society* (Oxford: Oxford University Press, 1969); William B. Moul, "On Getting Nothing for Something: A Note on Causal Models of Political Development," *Comparative Political Studies* 7, no. 2 (July 1974); Donald E. Smith, *Religion and Political Development* (Boston: Little, Brown, and Company, 1970); and Myron Weiner, ed., *Modernization: The Dynamics of Growth* (New York: Basic Books, 1966).

4. Peter Berger, Brigitte Berger, and Hansfried Kellner, *The Homeless Mind: Modernization and Consciousness* (New York: Random House, 1973), p. 9. I have relied on this book for the terms used to discuss modernization throughout this chapter.

5. Ibid.

6. Ibid., p. 12.

7. Ibid., p. 26.

8. Ibid., p. 29.

9. Ibid., p. 35.

10. Ibid., p. 39.

11. Paul M. Harrison, *Authority and Power in the Free Church Tradition: A Social Case Study of the American Baptist Convention* (Carbondale, Ill.: Southern Illinois University Press, 1959), p. 102.

12. Ibid., p. 129.

13. Ibid., p. 227.

14. Ibid., p. 207.

15. Ibid.

16. Berger, *The Homeless Mind*, pp. 83-96; and Lionel Trilling, *Sincerity and Authenticity* (Cambridge: Harvard University Press, 1972).

17. Martin Luther King, Jr., *Where Do We Go From Here: Chaos or Community?* (New York: Bantam Books, 1967), p. 51.

18. Ibid., p. 114.

19. Ibid., p. 118.

20. Ibid., p. 200.

21. Ibid., p. 222.

22. Ibid., p. 43.

23. Stokely Carmichael and Charles V. Hamilton, *Black Power: The Politics of Liberation in America* (New York: Random House, 1967).

24. Berger, *The Homeless Mind*, pp. 79-80.

9

SPIRITUAL RENEWAL AS CULTURAL REVITALIZATION

The forces of technology, bureaucracy, and urbanization have not lessened in contemporary America. Indeed, the question now is whether such modernizing forces can be harnessed to humane goals, or whether they will carry modern people—while promising "the good life"—ever further from their inner dreams. As government, industry, business, the military, cities, and mass media continue to grow, social life becomes increasingly impersonal. Individuality becomes a private matter; personal freedom is expressed not in public action but in various subjective adventures. Meaning ("where it's at") is increasingly private ("in your head"). The privatization of consciousness puts new pressures on, and creates new possibilities for, religion.

Many areas of social life have been liberated from religious control. Education, law, the state, and the economy have been secularized, and the church does not orient the modern city as it did the town square. While the kind of God associated with an older way of being religious may appear to have "died," the retreat of religion from much of public life seems only to have intensified its power in the private realm. If God's image is not the Father transcendent over the external world of modernity, a divine presence has nevertheless come forth in a mass of inward spiritual phenomena. Modernization has made religion "invisible," but only for a time. The picture of modern man as autonomously "coming of age" in "the secular city" will no longer do. Outward modernization apparently makes men yearn for the inner sense of meaning and worth religion has traditionally provided. In any event, the 1970s witnessed numerous movements of spiritual renewal. It is too early to prognosticate their outward impact, but we can begin to understand the movements themselves.

From his study of non-Western cultures, anthropologist Anthony F. C. Wallace constructed, in 1956, a paradigm of "revitalization movements" that helps in interpreting contemporary American religion. Wallace suggests that religions get started when the members of a society undertake a deliberate, conscious, organized effort to construct a more satisfying culture.[1] Successful attempts to breathe new life into a society necessarily take time and generally evolve, according to Wallace's model, in a process with several overlapping stages. Initially, a society's existence is generally stable. There may be pressures and problems, but the society has effective ways of coping with stress and satisfying needs, and it has broadly accepted definitions of what constitutes deviancy. In time, though, various individuals may experience increasing stress as the conventional means of coping deteriorate in the face of climatic changes, military defeat, imposed acculturation, economic distress, epidemics, and the like. When stress spreads more widely, the society enters a period of cultural distortion. Various aspects of life become mutually inconsistent and interfere with one another. Some individuals experiment with new styles of life, others turn to such psychodynamically regressive innovations as "alcoholism, extreme passivity and indolence, the development of highly ambivalent dependency relationships, intragroup violence, disregard of kinship and sexual mores, irresponsibility in public officials, states of depression and self-reproach, and probably a variety of psychosomatic and neurotic disorders."[2] Such widespread disillusionment may presage the defeat or death of the society, or a period of revitalization, often religious in character, which must perform certain major tasks.

The person who becomes the prophet of the movement has moments of insight or revelation which reorganize and recombine various elements of society's common image of selfhood, culture, and society into a new pattern or "mazeway." Often a divine figure appears to the leader and explains that renewed attention to certain neglected rules, symbols, or practices will bring spiritual health and relieve social distress. The prophet or leader spreads the good news that those who identify with the new cultural system will be cared for by the divine figure and will benefit materially by adopting the new "mazeway." As the movement grows, its followers are organized, often with a small clique of close disciples surrounding the main prophet. Then comes a time of adaptation, when the "mazeway" is modified to meet new needs and to deal with resistance from intransigent elements in the society. As society accepts the movement, the entire culture is transformed. Cultural transformation revitalizes the society by reducing individual deterioration and linking renewed persons together in organized programs of action. As the reformed culture succeeds in reducing stress-generating situations, it becomes established as normal in various economic, social, and political institutions. Finally, the once radical movement is routinized. With its goals achieved, the movement now contracts its energies toward "the preservation of doctrine and the performance of ritual (i.e., it becomes a church)."[3]

Following the success of the revitalization movement, the society enters a new time of stability. Now social life is recognizably different from the earlier, stress-prone state, and is different also from the period of cultural distortion that precipitated the revitalization movement. Given the processive structure outlined above, Wallace offers a succinct definition: "The effort to work a change in mazeway [the mental image of society, culture, body, and self that everyone has] and 'real' [external] system together so as to permit more effective stress reduction is the effort at revitalization; and the collaboration of a number of persons in such an effort is called a revitalization movement."[4] Such movements, Wallace points out, may combine several goals: a nativistic elimination of aliens, a

revivalistic renewal of old ways, a "cargo cult" or vitalistic importation of foreign goods and values, a millenarian vision of social
transformation, and a messianic emphasis on a savior figure. However these elements are combined, the movement's success may be
assessed in the short run by its realism in conflict situations and in
the long run by its reduction of overall stress.

Wallace's paradigm is an ideal type—certain modifications
would be necessary for it to illuminate the specificity of any given
social situation. Given the requisite alterations, the idea of revitalization movements as religious processes of social change helps to
interpret the marketplace of competing spiritual options in contemporary America.

America has probably never known a "steady state." Thoughts
of a time when life was placid and coherent are only dreams. Historical scrutiny shows that life on a frontier farm, for example, was
far from bucolic. But the intensity of our current nostalgia for cultural "roots" does demonstrate the pervasively felt dislocation of
contemporary life. Although some may be quite at home in the current system, it is safe to say that what Wallace calls individual
stress and cultural distortion have characterized our recent past.

Thus, in the best judgment of its chief prophet Robert Bellah,
America's "civil religion" is now "in time of trial." His book—like a
Puritan jeremiad—is titled *The Broken Covenant*.[5] Social theorist
Robert Nisbet takes an even darker view, arguing in *Twilight of
Authority* that contemporary America bears "all of the major
stigmata" of a declining civilization—"cultural decay, erosion of
institutions, progressive inflation of values in all spheres, economic
included, and constantly increasing centralization—and militariza-
tion—of power." In Nisbet's vision of the twentieth-century West,
"over everything hangs the specter of war."[6] Bureaucratization
feeds on itself until public institutions threaten to wrap every aspect
of life in jumbles of red tape. Technology's amazing accomplish-
ments come at the price of reducing the capacity of the earth to sustain human life, say defenders of the natural environment. Urbanization creates ghettos of decay and despair. Mass communications
media romanticize violence and challenge sexual roles and family
patterns. The complaints are commonplace.

Certainly these are times for deliberate, conscious, organized efforts to construct a more satisfying culture. Wallace's paradigm suggests that signs of new life may surface as revitalization movements, and many such phenomena compete for the allegiance of contemporary Americans. The ecological and women's liberation movements, for example, function like religions but make few direct claims to substantive spirituality. As signs of social distress, these movements raise important concerns for religious people. In addition, a number of more substantively spiritual movements presage new ways of being religious in America.

The proponents of a welter of "new" religions have imported—primarily from Asia and the East—ideas and values alien to the American system of Protestant, Catholic, and Jew. According to Robert S. Ellwood, Jr., religious groups founded in America after the Second World War "tend to take to an extreme the basic alternative reality idea that the only God one can find is within and known only by expansion of interior awareness."[7] If the war made Americans more cosmopolitan, the new generation—especially in the 1960s—adopted Eastern religious symbols as a way of expressing their alienation from established American institutions. The spread of such faiths as Nichiren Shoshu, Zen, Subud, and Krishna Consciousness, "which almost rejoice in their foreignness,"[8] shows widespread dissatisfaction especially among American youth with the "triumphs" of modernity. It also demonstrates the power of modernization to make religion an increasingly private, inward affair.

Cataloging all of these imported religions would be an exhaustive task, and might prove to be misplaced ardor. The lasting effect of the current revival of an alternative reality tradition in America cannot be evaluated by the number of its converts. Instead, as Ellwood says, "their real triumphs" will come "in the changes they make in the tone of the whole culture, not least within the traditional churches and synagogues [sic] themselves."[9] With their paramount stress on "the interior realization of a new state of consciousness," these movements, as well as the responses to them, "show that we are in a time of spiritual change and creativity."[10] Eastern religions continue to express the spiritual alienation many people feel upon coming of age in America. But some of their basic tenets—the Buddhist belief, for example, that selfhood is an illusion and the desire for it the chief cause of human misery—are so foreign to Western traditions that they serve more to reject than to reformulate American mazeways toward revitalizing society. Nevertheless, the numerous cults and spiritual techniques recently imported from the East, especially given their coverage by the mass media, have made mainstream Americans more tolerant of unforeseen outbursts of spirituality, and more alert to voices from within.

More promising resources for the religious revitalization of American life are found in two movements known as Charismatic Renewal and the New Evangelicalism. Both are what Wallace would call revivalistic movements, since they seek to renew forgotten elements of the society's traditional religion, Protestant Christianity. Both have passed through some overlapping stages in the process of revitalization. Yet neither fits the paradigm with precision. Wallace's model illumines these movements; conversely, their failure to fit the model neatly highlights the distinctively pluralistic character of contemporary American culture.

From its beginnings in the 1950s, Charismatic Renewal has given its adherents a spiritually positive experience of the subjectivism and privatization so characteristic of religion in modernity. Like any vital religious movement, the experience has come in unexpected ways. The movement is defined by a recent expositor, Richard Quebedeaux:

> In principle, Charismatic Renewal is a "transdenominational" movement of enthusiastic Christianity that emerged and became recognizable in the "historic" denominations only in 1960. It is theologically diverse but generally orthodox, and is unified by a common experience—the baptism of the Holy Spirit—with accompanying *charismata* (Greek "gifts") to be used personally and corporately in the life of the church. Evangelistic in nature, the movement is also genuinely reformist in character, and is represented largely by persons from the middle and upper-middle socioeconomic levels of society.[11]

The "baptism of the Holy Spirit" which is the experiential core of the movement refers to an exuberant outburst of *glossolalia* ("speaking in tongues") that follows an intense session of prayer. Already a converted Christian, the person seeking spiritual baptism is usually aided by the prayers and physical contact of a small group of charismatics in a ritual called "the laying on of hands."

A resurgence of spiritual phenomena not seen on any wide scale since the early days of Christianity (described in the book of the Acts of the Apostles in the New Testament) certainly constitutes a conscious, deliberate, organized effort to reformulate the mazeway of contemporary society. As in the New Testament, contemporary charismatics recognize other "gifts," such as prophecy. But their emphasis is primarily on *glossolalia*. One person babbles in syllables heretofore unheard, while another employs his gift to interpret the message to the group. The experience, charismatics stress, lets them know God as a Person rather than an idea and imparts power and authenticity to their Christian faith.

Unlike a revitalization movement in a traditional society, there is no chief prophet or single leader in Charismatic Renewal. The movement sprang up democratically, and its primary emphasis has continued to be on spreading the baptism of the spirit to individual Christians, rather than on implementing the vision of a main leader. Charismatic Renewal has been communicated throughout America and also around the world. Its message has been just what Wallace described—that its converts are cared for by God and will benefit materially from their experience. As an advertisement for *Charisma* magazine put it, "It's God's will for you to prosper if you meet the biblical prerequisites. We told you how to 'give the Master charge of your finances.' "

Describing an earlier revival in the "burned-over district" of New York, historian Whitney Cross noted that "once the spasm commenced, elaborate precautions were aimed at preventing untoward incidents and at sharpening and deepening fervor." For example, "fanatics, hypocrites, or persons too inarticulate to impress people of good taste" were discouraged from participating.[12] True to form, instead of sacrificing their possessions or engaging in practices beneath their social status, contemporary charismatics repeatedly emphasize their affluence and respectability. Their insistence on dropping such cultural baggage as the "holy rolling" of early twentieth-century Pentecostals has exposed contemporary charismatics to some ridicule from more conservative Christians. As one reviewer put it, "you can now speak in tongues and still enjoy martinis at the country club. Pentecostalism has come a long way, baby."[13] But for the charismatics themselves, the linkage between spiritual experience and affluent social status confirms the rightness of the movement.

While their organization has not taken the institutional form of traditional revitalization movements, a group of leaders has emerged within Charismatic Renewal. As in all things, experiential authority is the prime requisite for leadership. Persons with previously achieved social status—such as entertainers or politicians— join ministers and priests in a loose association of leadership. When they are not successful executives, the movement's leaders are often supported by members of organizations such as the Full Gospel Business Men's Fellowship International. As the television broadcasts of former tentmeeting-faith-healer-turned-university-president Oral Roberts show, the leaders of the movement use mass communications media most effectively.

In dealing with resistance from established denominations and churches, Charismatic Renewal has negotiated what Wallace calls the adaptation stage of a revitalization movement. Rather than retreating and forming their own denomination, contemporary charismatics have consistently worked to renew existing churches. Leaders like Dennis Bennett, whose participation in the movement caused his removal in 1960 from the rectorship of St. Mark's Episcopal Church in Van Nuys, California, have urged their followers to continue their membership and to work as spiritual leaven in their churches. Sometimes charismatic prayer groups are formed within churches, and sometimes church members join a charismatic group while continuing to work in their own churches. This is reminiscent of the nonseparating Puritans' desire to purify and enliven existing religious institutions. Their tenacity and resilience in this respect have won today's charismatics the gradual approval of churches including the Roman Catholics, United Presbyterians, and Assemblies of God.

Evidently Charismatic Renewal is entering what Wallace describes as the stage of cultural transformation. The movement has been effective in reducing the sense of malaise its members had previously experienced. And it appears to be enabling spiritual communication—but little institutionalized ecumenicity—between the various Christian churches. But the movement has not yet undertaken any significant group action programs for major social change. Indeed here its emphasis on respectability, affluence, and culture approval may undercut its power as a full-scale revitalization movement. Journalist Jean Stone in 1964 suggested rules of conduct which Quebedeaux says "reflect the normative Neo-Pentecostal position today":

> Speaking in tongues is not spooky; it's wholesome, good, clean, beautiful. We use no weird positions, no peculiar gymnastics. Don't add your little goodies to it. If you make it sound peculiar, you'll scare people pea-green. I remember one pastor's wife moaned, and it scared my husband to death! Don't moan or shriek. Remember, the gift is to edify and shrieking isn't edifying. And beware of personal prophecy, or prophecy about catastrophic happenings. If we seem too strange to outsiders, we're not going to get many outsiders to become insiders. You'll only attract desperate people. Don't develop separatist tendencies. Instead we are trying to save souls and be witness [sic] for Christ in what we say and in the way we live. And don't make the Bible a magical thing; be grounded in the Bible, but don't be a Bible thumper.[14]

This attitude suggests that Charismatic Renewal may remain a one-sided revitalization movement, never attempting to match its reformulation of contemporary "mazeways" with changes in the "real," external social structure.

Without inducing fairly sweeping social changes, Charismatic Renewal will certainly not face the routinization that is the final stage of Wallace's model. But in another sense, the movement may have become routine for its adherents, if not for the society as a whole. Fully understanding the role of this movement requires another examination of what cultural pluralism means for religion. But first we should look at another, somewhat similar current revitalization movement, the "New Evangelicalism."

Today's Evangelical movement appears to differ from Charismatic Renewal primarily in its concentration upon conversion rather than baptism in the spirit and *glossolalia*. The New Evangelicalism was a large movement even before it was noticed by the mass media. Jim Wallis gives a good description:

> I remember a hot muggy night in Dallas, Texas, during the summer of 1972. I was sitting in the Cotton Bowl among a handful of news reporters who were on hand to cover Explo '72, an evangelistic extravaganza put on by Campus Crusade for Christ. It was an evening meeting and 100,000 evangelical young people were being led in what were called "Jesus Cheers." All index fingers were raised high in the air and the huge crowd began to chant, "One way, One way, One way," in a deafening unison that seemed to shake the whole stadium.
>
> One reporter, who seemed almost overwhelmed with a mixture of fear and utter bewilderment, turned to me and asked, "Who are these people? Where do they come from? How could anything this big have happened without us (the press) knowing anything about it?" Very few reporters from the so-called "secular-press" were in attendance at Explo '72. Those who came were not prepared for what they witnessed in Dallas.
>
> I tried to explain . . . that evangelical Christians were a subculture in America, perhaps one of the very few subcultures left in the country. I told him how evangelicals have their own churches, their own organizations, their own schools, their own publications, their own leaders, their own financial support, and their own communications network—a formal and informal grapevine tying it all together. I described to him how the news, information, ideas, money, people, and popular wisdom of the evangelical world all circulate via that vast communications network, right under the noses of the secular press and media watchdogs. It was the enormous size and efficiency of this subcultural network which explained how something as large as Explo '72 took the media by surprise.[15]

Although more effectively organized and institutionalized than the charismatics, the New Evangelicals too are primarily concerned with a singular religious experience—conversion. Like the Charismatics, these converts learn that God cares personally for them and that they will benefit materially from their conversion.

Since the 1976 Presidential election of Jimmy Carter—a confessing evangelical Christian—extensive media attention has given the new Evangelicals overt cultural influence. At the 1977 annual meeting of the National Association of Evangelicals, the program coordinator, evangelist Dave Breeze, exulted: "It no longer fits to picture us as redneck preachers pounding the pulpit. Evangelical Christianity has become the greatest show on earth. Twenty to forty years ago it was on the edge of things. Now it has moved to the center." The organization's executive director, Billy Melvin, agreed: "The major pulpits are ours. Our schools are full, our churches are growing, our publishing houses are flourishing . . . financially we are on solid ground. . . . Ours is an emergence that cannot be stopped."[16] Coverage by the mass media has caused some Evangelicals to accept many of the cultural symbols and values that the media have monitored and created.

Status and attention may tempt Evangelicals to affirm success more than separation from their society. As Wallis notes, for example:

> Marabel Morgan has a new message for evangelical women, so long cloistered and told that sex was dirty. Now they can be "total women" who are successful sex symbols, skillful manipulators and conquerors of male ego, under the guise of wifely submissiveness to husbands and all justified in the name of Christian principles. Evangelical wives and single women can now look like Hollywood starlets and feel good about it. No more fundamentalist prohibitions against make-up, fashionable wardrobes, or sexy outfits.[17]

Yet some Evangelicals believe that the experience of conversion leads directly into group action programs for social change. Claiming to represent a "Moral Majority," some Evangelicals captured media attention and influenced local, state, and national political races in 1980. They directed public attention backward toward the individualistic virtues of an earlier, politically conservative "Christian America." Sounding a less strident, more progressive note, the readers of *Sojourners* magazine and members of Evangelicals for Social Action indicate their movement may, in addition to reformulating individual "mazeways," also attempt to work changes in the "real," external structures of society. It is at least possible that the new Evangelicals will enter what Wallace calls the stage of cultural transformation and that theirs may become a revitalization movement. Certainly some of the new Evangelicals are seeking to meet that challenge.

In their rejection of the image of modern man as autonomous, secular, and thoroughly rational, all of these recent spiritual movements are agents of what Peter Berger calls "countermodernization." In their enthusiasm for ecstatic experience, they are akin to many other movements in contemporary America—from the drug scene to women's liberation to the hedonism of the discoteque. Technology, bureaucracy, the pluralization of social life-worlds wrought by urbanization and the mass media—these primary carriers of modernization will not be stopped. In fact, the religious subjectivism they foster may only strengthen the drive of modernization. Certainly it rarely challenges modernity's hegemony in America's external, real world.

One has to wonder to what extent religious groups cater to what Tom Wolfe has aptly called "the new narcissism" of contemporary America. L. Ron Hubbard's Church of Scientology, for example, incorporates technological values and devices in its program of "personal development." The religious movements examined above, however, may have the resources to be genuinely revitalizing influences in modern society. They may not, like revitalization movements in traditional societies, lead to a new "steady state." To interpret their possibilities and limits, we must understand the role of religion in a pluralistic culture.

Several kinds of pluralism need to be distinguished. Ethnic pluralism refers to the existence of several racial or cultural groups within the same society. Given the diversity of the American Indian nations and tribes, one might say that America was ethnically pluralistic even before its European settlement. Certainly it was when the white men came, and more so when white men brought African slaves to the New World. With its history of immigration, America has become increasingly pluralistic.

Ethnic groups have participated with tremendous variety in the formation of an American culture. Some ethnic groups have been so disenfranchised from the wider culture that they have reverted to and maintained earlier religious heritages, either in their own native tradition or in their own historic version of Christianity. Acculturation has been uneven, and many people have responded to the facelessness of modern society by reinvoking ethnic ways. The richness of America's ethnic traditions ensures a continuing variety in American religious life.

In addition to the continuing importance of ethnic pluralism there is religious pluralism. Legalized in the Constitution and institutionalized in the denominational system, religious pluralism has been called America's distinctive contribution to the history of religion. The proliferation of sects, cults, and churches, together with the importation of foreign religions and the rediscovery of Black and native American religions, ensures that the bureaucratization of mainstream denominations and the emptiness of what Will Herberg calls the religion of "the American Way of Life" will not blot out this additional source of variety.[18]

Along with ethnic and religious pluralism, a full interpretation of the role of religion in American history requires an understanding of cultural pluralism. By cultural pluralism I mean the tendency of religion to align its energies with symbols and values from different aspects of life. Given the openness of experience in so vast a new world, ethnic and religious pluralism made it possible for religious experience to find expression in political, psychological, literary, and ethical symbols. As we have seen, the changing demands of history enabled religion to enter new and vital symbolic alignments in different episodes of American life.

The interworking of these three kinds of pluralism provides a clue to understanding not only the past but also the present role of religion. The Great Awakening of the 1730s and 1740s was a vital outburst of inward, psychological religious experience that ushered in the spiritual climate of the American Revolution. The Second Great Awakening of the early nineteenth century was another inward religious convulsion that brought new social institutions of denominationalism. The contemporary renewal of inward religious experience will be remembered as a "great" awakening only if it too proceeds not only to reformulate individual "mazeways," but also to revitalize the external world of American society.

Our history of cultural pluralism suggests that a fresh alignment of religion with other aspects of life—perhaps with environmental or economic concerns—is likely to occur. Speaking of religious transformations, Harvard Law professor Laurence H. Tribe conjectures that "the reintegration of reason and moral perception may be augured by the dawning of environmental awareness in contemporary law and culture."[19] And historian John F. Wilson foresees the emergence of international economic management as a new mode of resolving social stress and coping with cultural change.[20] An understanding of the variety of cultural roles religion has played in the past should alert us to some of the new forms religion may take. Some new synthesis will be necessary if religion is to be a vital force in contemporary America. The spiritual power of the new inwardness will have to break out in novel ways if the privatization of religion is not to end in subjective enthusiasm while our modern Rome burns. An understanding of historical diversity provides an occasion for openness to new religious vitality.

An awareness of the interworking of ethnic, religious, and cultural pluralism suggests both the limits and the possibilities of current movements of spiritual renewal. The continuing power of ethnic and religious pluralism indicates that no single religious movement will revitalize the entire range of American society. It would be a mistake to look for *the* new American religion. Ethnic and religious pluralism also suggest that we may see religion in concurrence with not only one but several aspects of life. Inward spiritual renewal may bring social reform for one ethnic or religious group, and political involvement or a new art form for another. Whatever happens, history instructs us to be alert for new revelations of the sacrality of life in all its aspects. The past can help us understand the present and, just possibly, open for us a new future.

NOTES

1. Anthony F. C. Wallace, "Revitalization Movements," *American Anthropologist* 58 (1956): 264-81, reprinted in abridged form in William A. Lessa and Evon Z. Vogt, *Reader in Comparative Religion: An Anthropological Approach* (New York: Harper and Row, 1956). The reference here is to Lessa and Vogt, p. 504.

2. Ibid., p. 507.

3. Ibid., p. 509.

4. Ibid., p. 505.

5. Robert N. Bellah, *The Broken Covenant: American Civil Religion in Time of Trial* (New York: Seabury Press, 1975).

6. Robert Nisbet, *Twilight of Authority* (New York: Oxford University Press, 1975), pp. vi, v.

7. Robert S. Ellwood, Jr., *Religious and Spiritual Groups in Modern America* (Englewood Cliffs, N.J.: Prentice-Hall, Inc., 1973), p. 83.

8. Ibid.

9. Ibid., p. 84.

10. Ibid., p. 297.

11. Richard Quebedeaux, *The New Charismatics: The Origins, Development, and Significance of Neo-Pentecostalism* (Garden City, N.Y.: Doubleday and Company, Inc., 1976), p. 5.

12. Whitney R. Cross, *The Burned-Over District* (New York: Harper and Row, 1965), pp. 176, 177.

13. John Cahoon, "From Status-Seeking . . . Good Lord, Deliver Us," *New Oxford Review* 45, no. 4 (April 1978): 19.

14. Quebedeaux, *The New Charismatics*, p. 152.

15. Jim Wallis, "The New Evangelicalism," *The Chicago Theological Seminary Register* 68, no. 1 (Winter 1978): 7.

16. Ibid., p. 8.

17. Ibid., p. 9.

18. Will Herberg, *Protestant-Catholic-Jew: An Essay in American Religious Sociology* (Garden City, N.Y.: Doubleday and Company, 1960), pp. 72-98.

19. Laurence H. Tribe, "Ways Not To Think About Plastic Trees: New Foundations for Environmental Law," *The Yale Law Journal* 83, no. 7 (July 1974): 1336.

20. John F. Wilson, *Public Religion in American Culture* (Philadelphia: Temple University Press, 1979), pp. 172-75.

10

EPILOGUE: RELIGION AND AMERICAN CULTURAL HISTORY

My emphasis on the fresh wineskins, or the new cultural forms of religion in different episodes in American life, presumes a certain understanding of the nature of religion. As Edwin S. Gaustad, Darline Miller, and G. Allison Stokes have said:

> The study of religion in America (or anywhere else) is guided not by a single method but by a single, albeit bafflingly complex, subject matter. "Religious Studies," like "American Studies," draws from or adapts itself to many disciplines, methodologies, and perspectives.[1]

The variousness of perspective involved in the preceding narrative is an attempt to do justice to the complexity of religion and culture. Now that my narrative is complete, I want to spell out more precisely what I mean by "religion" and "culture," and then to point out some of the implications—and limitations—of my approach.

If culture is the web of meanings through which humans have personal and social being, then religion may be understood as the way people symbolically express their culture's relation to a primordial, fundamental order or ground of reality, often imaged as a divine being. As an anchor of meaning, religion touches, at one time or another, virtually all of human experience and every form of human social interaction. To comprehend this basic aspect of life, our overall perspective has to be cultural—a perspective that takes account of religion's various substantive and functional characteristics. We need to consider both the nature of religion (its substance) and also the role of religion in relation to other aspects and elements of human life (its functions).

Religious spokesmen and scholars have tried to define the nature of religion as a phenomenon in its own right. They have attempted to speak in terms appropriate to the meaning and truth people have discovered in religious experience. Some have tried, as it were, to let religious phenomena "speak" for themselves. Such an attempt is clearly of vital importance, but it suffers an inherent temptation. Attempts to define religion substantively are almost always colored by the character of the particular religion under consideration, or by the religious allegiance of the commentator. Perplexed by the absence of God in Buddhism or the plethora of deities in Hinduism, Christian theologians have called them "pagan" and declared theirs the true religion.

There is much to be said for a substantive approach. But such definitional imperialism is of little use to students of religion as an aspect of human life. One way to preserve the vitality of a substantive point of view without falling prey to the terms of any particular sect is to investigate religion as a shared apprehension of, or attitude toward, life as grounded in and bounded by a sacred reality which transcends and supports the human and secures its ultimate meaning and worth. Such a working definition should enable us to attend sensitively to the substantive nature of many religions— even religion in modern America.

Many scholars, however, have noted that substantive approaches fail to account for the ways religion enters into other aspects of human life. By looking at what religion does rather than asking what it is, such scholars adopt a functional perspective. Cultural anthropologist Clifford Geertz, for example, studies religion as a "cultural system" by investigating how its symbols motivate people and regulate all sorts of activities.[2] Such an approach avoids the temptations toward definitional imperialism involved in many substantive approaches. Examining individual and social behavior in the light of symbols and motivations enables us to see how religion is intrinsically related to other aspects of human life. To achieve a sound and comprehensive interpretation of religion, then, we need a perspective which combines substantive and functional approaches. We need, as it were, to keep both eyes open.

As we have seen, religion has several basic elements, any one or several of which may predominate at a given time or in a particular cultural climate. If we want to interpret religion as an aspect of life, we must keep them all in mind. Isolating them for the purpose of specification, the elements of religion include:

1. individual, "internal" experience
2. social behavior—within specifically religious groups and vis-à-vis society as a whole
3. guidelines for individual and social moral action
4. sources of meaning and explanation—revelations of supernatural powers or divine figures in sacred texts and myths
5. mental reflection—philosophical examination of the grounds of religion, thought about the nature and meaning of religion, and theological work within particular communities of faith
6. relations with other symbolic or imaginative projects, such as the arts, in a given culture.

Any of these qualities may dominate the configuration at a certain time, but soon the various elements shift into new alignments. Religion is an aspect of human *life*.

Understanding its diversity and its vitality underscores the appropriateness of cultural history as a way of studying religion. But we should recognize several problems facing the cultural historian of religion. There is always the problem of achieving a view of the past which is both accurate historically and usable in the present. This problem is more serious than it sounds, because almost all of the past is inherently usable and because it is difficult for any historian to write without contemporary issues molding—if unconsciously—the way material is organized. Awareness of this problem can free us from illusions of pristine objectivity and from skewing the past for the sake of contemporary relevance.

To some extent, everyone's own time seems more complicated than the "simplicity" of previous periods of history. Distance of time and place allows us to categorize the basic elements of other cultural traditions with an exactness we would resist closer to home. Our need for useful interpretations of other times heightens this temptation. Yet if we resist the temptation to neatly label the vital currents and mixed dimensions of our own experience, we ought to be equally fair to the people and cultures we subject to historical scrutiny. The past can actually be useful in our present spiritual lives if we honestly understand previous ways of being religious. We need to know how religion has been expressed in American history if we want to interpret its alignment with other aspects of life today. The patterns of the past can alert us to what is authentically enduring, or novel, in contemporary religion.

Another problem for the cultural historian of religion in America is this country's ineluctable modernity. Despite their arguments about the exact nature of such primary forces as technology, bureaucracy, and urbanization, social scientists and humanists agree that a fundamental change in human life has occurred comparable to the agricultural revolution or the emergence of early city-state civilizations. Historians may debate whether modernization began two or three or four hundred years ago, but they probably agree that its forces continue to influence American life. Modernity raises so many questions about religion that traditional approaches to religion seem too theological, too restrictively ecclesiastical, too ethnocentric. Cultural analysis may not answer all of our questions. But by paying attention to how religion is manifest in diverse ways and forms through time, we are more able to interpret the nature of religion in modern life.

America's intrinsic pluralism is one more complicating factor for the cultural historian. If white European immigrants sought hegemony by converting—or, more commonly, displacing or annihilating—the Indians of North America, they ironically ensured the development of an ethnically pluralistic society by importing

African slaves. Immigrants from throughout Europe and other continents kept America's population mixed. Even among such relatively homogeneous ethnic groups as the English, religious differences soon emerged in the New World. Despite fantastic efforts, American culture has never been "pure." In addition to ethnic diversity and religious variety, different religious orientations have come to life in important episodes in American history. Religion has been in close alignment with various aspects of life: political, social, psychological, artistic and ethical. Any attempt to tell the whole story of religion as an aspect of American life will have to focus on the interworking of ethnic, religious, and cultural pluralism.

I have accented the role of cultural pluralism not because it is most important but because it seems to have been the most neglected. Herein lie the most telling limitations of my approach. Concentrating on the dominant tradition of white Protestant Christianity illustrates the working of cultural pluralism in the clearest available terms. This mainline tradition has shaped and been formed by other, equally important traditions. But the religious stories of black, Indian, and Spanish-speaking Americans, the stories of Roman Catholics and Jews, and the stories of women within all of these traditions, should not be forced by the historian to conform to the contours of the mainline story.

These other traditions also have expressed their religious experience in a variety of cultural forms—not necessarily in the same ways, or at the same times—as the dominant tradition. To take one example, Nathan Glazer has pointed out that

> to every generation of recent times a different part of the Jewish past has become meaningful. At the same time, to be sure, other parts of that tradition, great chunks without which it seems it must die, were rejected. And yet at no point has everything been rejected at once; a kind of shifting balance has been maintained whereby each generation could relate itself meaningfully to some part of the Jewish past.[3]

Glazer argues that the pattern of American Judaism differs from Protestant Christianity in that it is centered around a sense of community rather than belief and experience.[4] This means that "the periodization of Jewish history is not the periodization of general history, nor is the periodization of American Jewish history that of American history."[5] Thus while an important chapter in the mainline story is "the political faith of '76," religion and politics came together most closely for American Jews during the Holocaust and again in the Israeli war of 1967.[6] Looking squarely at such differences points out the limits of the mainline story and also underscores the importance of cultural pluralism in the religious histories of all Americans.

Finally, I want to point out that an awareness of the significance of American cultural pluralism means that a sense of the wholeness of life in all of its dimensions, which many people take to be the essence of religion, is available through the process of historical interpretation. I do not think that consciousness of cultural pluralism necessarily cuts us off from the possibility of genuinely new religious experience. In fact, such knowledge may sensitize us to be open to religious revelations in unexpected areas of life. But an awareness of cultural pluralism should also help us to maintain a healthy, critical perspective on new religious visions. The facts of cultural pluralism remind us that no single form of religion expresses all of life's ultimate meaning. Such an insight may also enable us not only to criticize but also to deepen our own spiritual experience by comparing it with other cultural forms of religion. Historical interpretation, then, may enhance our understanding and also enrich our faith.

NOTES

1. Edwin S. Gaustad, Darline Miller, and G. Allison Stokes, "Religion in America," *American Quarterly* 31, no. 3 (1979 Bibliography Issue): 250.

2. Clifford Geertz, *The Interpretation of Cultures* (New York: Basic Books, Inc., 1973), pp. 87-125.

3. Nathan Glazer, *American Judaism*, 2d ed., rev. (Chicago: The University of Chicago Press, 1972), p. 142.

4. Ibid., p. 148.

5. Ibid., p. 151.

6. Ibid., p. 155.

BIBLIOGRAPHIC ESSAY

The citations in this essay are not meant to appear exhaustive or even "complete" with respect to the history of religion in America. The best place to begin is with the two volumes of Nelson R. Burr's *A Critical Bibliography of Religion in America* (Princeton: Princeton University Press, 1961). Readers seeking a more manageable list, which still covers the basic works on many traditions and periods, should consult the bibliography in Sydney E. Ahlstrom's *A Religious History of the American People* (New Haven, Conn.: Yale University Press, 1972). Henry Warner Bowden's *Dictionary of American Religious Biography* (Westport, Conn.: Greenwood Press, 1977) is an invaluable source of information about a wide variety of interesting individuals.

I simply want to guide readers to the historical and theoretical sources for each of my chapters. Hence the citations and comments that follow deal with the choices I made in telling this particular story. Each episode is complex; a full understanding of its events requires much more historical narrative than any one of my chapters includes, and a thorough interpretation of religion in a particular episode needs the illumination of additional perspectives. If readers are led to undertake more intensive historical study and to consider the use of a variety of analytic perspectives, the goal of this book will have been reached—to inspire readers to go beyond it.

PREFACE

Several recent articles speak directly to the need for a variety of disciplinary perspectives for the interpretation of religion in American history:

Gaustad, Edwin S.; Miller, Darline; and Stokes, G. Allison. "Religion in America." *American Quarterly* 31, no. 3 (Bibliography Issue, 1979): 250-83.

Michaelsen, Robert S. "Review of *A History of the Churches in the United States and Canada*, by Robert T. Handy." *Religious Studies Review* 4, no. 2 (April 1978): 101-4.

Wilson, John F. "A Review of Some Reviews." Review of reviews of *A Religious History of the American People*, by Sydney E. Ahlstrom. *Religious Studies Review* 1, no. 1 (September 1975): 1-8.

CHAPTER 1

For a theoretical discussion of the interpretive perspective of this chapter the reader is encouraged to consult Mircea Eliade's *The Sacred and the Profane: The Nature of Religion* (New York: Harcourt, Brace & World, Inc., 1959) and Mary Douglas's *Natural Symbols: Explorations in Cosmology* (New York: Random House, 1970).

As an introduction to the Puritans' writings, the reader should see the two volumes edited by Perry Miller and Thomas H. Johnson, *The Puritans: A Sourcebook of Their Writings* (New York: Harper & Row, 1963). As a general historical work, Alan Simpson's *Puritanism in Old and New England* (Chicago: University of Chicago Press, 1955) remains a classic. Perry Miller's *Errand Into the Wilderness* (Cambridge: Harvard University Press, 1956) still provides the best succinct analysis of the Puritan's theological intentions; however, readers should note the additional aspects of Puritanism studied in the works surveyed by Michael McGiffert's in "American Puritan Studies in the 1960s" *William and Mary Quarterly*, Third Series, 27 (1970):36-67. Additional new analyses are given in the essays edited by Sacvan Bercovitch as *The American Puritan Imagination: Essays in Revaluation* (Cambridge: Cambridge University Press, 1974), and in Bercovitch's own works, *The Puritan Origins of the American Self* (New Haven: Yale University Press, 1975) and *The American Jeremiad* (Madison: University of Wisconsin Press, 1978). Winton U. Solberg provides an extensive study of one important Puritan ritual in *Redeem the Time: The Puritan Sabbath in Early America* (Cambridge: Harvard University Press, 1977), and David Leverenz gives a psychological analysis of how the Puritans responded to various tensions in *The Language of Puritan Feeling:*

An Exploration in Literature, Psychology, and Social History (New Brunswick: Rutgers University Press, 1980). Readers interested in the life of John Cotton may begin with Larzer Ziff's *The Career of John Cotton: Puritanism and the American Experience* (Princeton: Princeton University Press, 1962).

CHAPTER 2

Several recent articles survey current thinking and resources in the psychology of religion:

Bregman, Lucy. "Religion and Psychology: Recent Scholarship." *Religious Studies Review* 5, no. 2 (April 1979): 111-16.

Spilka, Bernard. "The Current State of the Psychology of Religion." *Bulletin of the Council on the Study of Religion* 9, no. 4 (October 1978): 66-69.

Stokes, G. Allison. "Bibliographies of Psychology/Religion Studies." *Religious Studies Review* 4, no. 4 (October 1978): 273-79.

Sigmund Freud's views on religion may be found in *The Future of an Illusion* (Garden City: Doubleday & Company, Inc., 1961) and *Civilization and Its Discontents* (New York: W. W. Norton and Company, Inc., 1961). Carl Jung's ideas about religion may be found in *Modern Man in Search of a Soul* (New York: Harcourt, Brace & World, Inc., 1933) and *Four Archetypes* (Princeton: Princeton University Press, 1959). Sources for the ideas of William James utilized in this chapter are his *The Varieties of Religious Experience* (New York: Macmillan Publishing Company, Inc., 1961) and *Essays on Faith and Morals* (New York: The New American Library, Inc., 1962). Interesting new work in the psychology of religion has been done by Paul W. Pruyser in *A Dynamic Psychology of Religion* (New York: Harper & Row, 1968) and *Between Belief and Unbelief* (New York: Harper & Row, 1974).

For general historical knowledge of the Great Awakening, the reader should consult:

Brauer, Jerald C. "Conversion: From Puritanism to Revivalism." *The Journal of Religion* 58, no. 3 (July 1978): 227-43.

Bushman, Richard L. *From Puritan to Yankee: Character and the Social Order in Connecticut, 1690-1765.* Cambridge: Harvard University Press, 1967.

Gaustad, Edwin S. *The Great Awakening in New England.* New York: Harper & Row, 1957.

Heimert, Alan. *Religion and the American Mind: From the Great Awakening to the Revolution.* Cambridge: Harvard University Press, 1966.

Readers who want a more concise survey of the writings of Jonathan Edwards than is afforded by the present and forthcoming volumes of his works published by Yale University Press should read the revised edition of Clarence Faust and Thomas J. Johnson's *Jonathan Edwards: Representative Selections* (New York: Hill and Wang, 1962) or Ola E. Winslow's *Jonathan Edwards: Basic Writings* (New York: The New American Library, Inc., 1966). Conrad Cherry's *The Theology of Jonathan Edwards: A Reappraisal* (Garden City: Doubleday & Company, Inc., 1966) and Perry Miller's *Jonathan Edwards* (New York: William Sloan Associates, 1949) are good studies of his thought, as are the chapters and essays on Edwards found in:

Ahlstrom, Sydney E. *Theology in America: The Major Protestant Voices from Puritanism to Neo-Orthodoxy.* Indianapolis: The Bobbs-Merrill Company, Inc., 1967.

————. *A Religious History of the American People.* New Haven: Yale University Press, 1972.

Clebsch, William A. *American Religious Thought: A History.* Chicago: University of Chicago Press, 1973.

Levin, David, ed. *Jonathan Edwards: A Profile.* New York: Hill and Wang, 1969.

Miller, Perry. *Errand Into the Wilderness.* Cambridge: Harvard University Press, 1956.

CHAPTER 3

The idea of political religion in less developed countries is introduced in David C. Apter's "Political Religion in the New Nations," in Clifford Geertz's *Old Societies and New States: The Quest for Modernity in Asia and Africa* (New York: The Free Press of Glencoe, 1963). Donald Eugene Smith explores the idea more fully in *Religion and Political Development* (Boston: Little, Brown and Company, 1970). Such an idea of religion is examined and critiqued in Frederick J. Streng, Charles L. Lloyd, Jr., and Jay T. Allen, *Ways of Being Religious: Readings for a New Approach to Religion* (Englewood Cliffs: Prentice-Hall, Inc., 1973), pp. 1-22, 417-80.

Two essays by Edmund S. Morgan examine the relationship between religion and politics in the Revolutionary Era: "The Puritan Ethic and the American Revolution," *William and Mary Quarterly*, Third Series 24, no.

4 (October 1967): 3-43, and "The Revolutionary Era as an Age of Politics," in John R. Howe, Jr.'s *The Role of Ideology in the American Revolution* (New York: Holt, Rinehart and Winston, 1970). An overview of these issues is given in the essays edited by Jerald C. Brauer as *Religion and the American Revolution* (Philadelphia: Fortress Press, 1976). Cushing Stout's *The New Heavens and New Earth: Political Religion in America* (New York: Harper and Row, 1974) and Catharine Albanese's *Sons of the Fathers* (Philadelphia: Temple University Press, 1976) are book-length treatments of the general topic. The implications of the interaction of religion and politics for the Christian churches are investigated more specifically in Nathan O. Hatch's *The Sacred Cause of Liberty: Republican Thought and the Millennium in Revolutionary New England* (New Haven: Yale University Press, 1977); Alan Heimert's *Religion and the American Mind: From the Great Awakening to the Revolution* (Cambridge: Harvard University Press, 1966); H. Richard Niebuhr's *The Kingdom of God in America* (New York: Harper & Row, 1937), pp. 88-126; and Mark C. Noll's *Christians in the American Revolution* (Washington: Christian University Press, 1977).

The best single-volume general history of the period is Gordon S. Wood's *The Creation of the American Republic, 1776-1787* (New York: W. W. Norton and Company, Inc., 1969). It can profitably be supplemented by Kenneth A. Lockridge's "Social Change and the Meaning of the American Revolution," *Journal of Social History* 6, no. 4 (Summer 1973): 403-39, and by the essays edited by Stephen G. Kurtz and James H. Hutson in *Essays on the American Revolution* (New York: W. W. Norton & Company, Inc., 1973). Bernard Bailyn's *The Ideological Origins of the American Revolution* (Cambridge: The Belknap Press, Harvard University Press, 1976) studies the importance of republican thought. *The Book of Abigail and John: Selected Letters of the Adams Family, 1762-1784*, edited by L. H. Butterfield, Marc Friedlaender, and Mary-Jo Kline (Cambridge: Harvard University Press, 1975), gives an inside view from the perspective of some illustrious participants.

Peter Gay's *The Enlightenment: An Interpretation, The Rise of Modern Paganism* (New York: Random House, 1966) does the excellent job for the Enlightenment in Europe that Henry F. May's *The Enlightenment in America* (New York: Oxford University Press, 1976) does for America. May's book can be supplemented by two articles from the special Summer 1976, issue of *American Quarterly*: Joseph Ellis, "Habits of Mind and an American Enlightenment," pp. 150-64, and D. H. Meyer, "The Uniqueness of the American Enlightenment," pp. 165-86.

Russell E. Richey and Donald G. Jones have collected the main documents of the "civil religion" debate in *American Civil Religion* (New York: Harper & Row, 1974). Robert N. Bellah's subsequent reflections are put forward in *The Broken Covenant: American Civil Religion in Time of Trial* (New York: The Seabury Press, 1975). John F. Wilson has recently clarified the substance and import of the "civil religion" proposals in *Public Religion in American Culture* (Philadelphia: Temple University Press, 1979).

CHAPTER 4

Two of the classic works in the sociology of religion are Max Weber's *The Sociology of Religion*, with an Introduction by Talcott Parsons (Boston: Beacon Press, 1963; first published in 1922) and Joachim Wach's *Sociology of Religion* (Chicago: University of Chicago Press, 1944). The essays edited by Robert W. Green as *Protestantism and Capitalism: The Weber Thesis and Its Critics* (Boston: Heath, 1959) examine the relationship between religion and economic institutions in the development of modern society. Peter L. Berger's *The Sacred Canopy: Elements of a Sociological Theory of Religion* (Garden City: Doubleday & Company, Inc., 1967) utilizes theories from the sociology of knowledge and has become something of a contemporary classic in the field. Gerhard E. Lenski's *The Religious Factor: A Study of Religion's Impact on Politics, Economics, and Family Life* (Garden City: Doubleday & Company, Inc., 1961) and Thomas Luckmann's *The Invisible Religion: The Problem of Religion in Modern Society* (New York: The Macmillan Company, Inc., 1967) join Berger's work as important contemporary studies.

Denominationalism, as the institutional shape of religion in America, is introduced well by the essays collected by Russell E. Richey in *Denominationalism* (Nashville: Abingdon Press, 1977). H. Richard Niebuhr's *The Social Sources of Denominationalism* (New York: Henry Holt and Company, Inc., 1929) was a pioneering sociological work and has continued to be valuable. It can now be supplemented with Andrew M. Greeley's *The Denominational Society* (Glenview, Ill.: Scott, Foresman, 1972).

For an introduction to revivalism in this period, the reader should see William Warren Sweet's *Revivalism in America: Its Origin, Growth and Decline* (New York: Charles Scribner's Sons, 1944) and Timothy L. Smith's *Revivalism and Social Reform in Mid-Nineteenth Century America* (New York: Abingdon Press, 1957). Additionally valuable studies include John Boles's *The Great Revival, 1787-1805: The Origins of the Southern Evangelical Mind* (Lexington: University of Kentucky Press, 1972); Whitney R. Cross's *The Burned-Over District: The Social and Intellectual History of Enthusiastic Religion in Western New York, 1800-1850* (Ithaca: Cornell

University Press, 1950); Martin E. Marty's *Righteous Empire: The Protestant Experience in America* (New York: The Dial Press, 1970), pp. 35-99; T. Scott Miyakawa's *Protestants and Pioneers: Individualism and Conformity on the American Frontier* (Chicago: University of Chicago Press, 1964); and Rhodes Thompson's editing of *Voices From Cane Ridge* (St. Louis: Bethany Press, 1954).

The essays edited by John F. Wilson as *Church and State in American History* (Boston: Heath, 1965) place the religious developments of this period in the framework of the "great experiment" of religious freedom.

CHAPTER 5

The essays edited and introduced by Nathan A. Scott, Jr. as *The New Orpheus: Essays Toward a Christian Poetic* (New York: Sheed & Ward, 1964) and by Giles Gunn as *Literature and Religion* (London: SCM Press, Ltd., 1971), when taken together, provide a sound introduction to the interdisciplinary study of religion and imaginative literature. Giles Gunn's *The Interpretation of Otherness: Literature, Religion, and the American Imagination* (New York: Oxford University Press, 1979); Robert Detweiler's *Story, Sign, and Self: Phenomenology and Structuralism as Literary-Critical Methods* (Philadelphia: Fortress Press, 1978); Wesley A. Kort's *Narrative Elements and Religious Meanings* (Philadelphia: Fortress Press, 1975); and Nathan A. Scott, Jr.'s *The Broken Center: Studies in the Theological Horizon of Modern Literature* (New Haven: Yale University Press, 1966) provide good examples of the variety of work in this interdisciplinary field.

The primary works from this period, discussed or mentioned in this chapter, include:

Emerson, Ralph Waldo. *The Selected Writings of Ralph Waldo Emerson.* Edited by Brooks Atkinson. New York: The Modern Library, 1964.

Hawthorne, Nathaniel. *The Scarlet Letter: A Romance.* Indianapolis: The Bobbs-Merrill Company, Inc., 1963.

Melville, Herman. *Moby-Dick; or, The Whale.* Indianapolis: The Bobbs-Merrill Company, Inc., 1964.

Thoreau, Henry David. *Walden and Civil Disobedience.* Edited by Owen Thomas. New York: W. W. Norton & Company, Inc., 1966.

Secondary sources for the imaginative writers of this period are legion. I recommend the following studies on these writers' contributions to the culture of Transcendentalism:

Barbour, Brian M., ed. *American Transcendentalism: An Anthology of Criticism*. Notre Dame: University of Notre Dame Press, 1973.

Boller, Paul F. *American Transcendentalism, 1830-1860: An Intellectual Inquiry*. New York: G. P. Putnam's Sons, 1974.

Buell, Lawrence. *Literary Transcendentalism: Style and Vision in the American Renaissance*. Ithaca: Cornell University Press, 1973.

Koster, Donald N. *Transcendentalism in America*. Boston: Twayne Publishers, 1975.

Matthiessen, F. O. *American Renaissance: Art and Expression in the Age of Emerson and Whitman*. New York: Oxford University Press, 1941.

Tanner, Tony. *The Reign of Wonder: Naivety and Reality in American Literature*. Cambridge: Cambridge University Press, 1965.

CHAPTER 6

The essays edited by Gene Outka and John P. Reeder as *Religion and Morality* (Garden City: Anchor Press, 1973) provide a good introduction to recent religious ethics. In *Can Ethics Be Christian?* (Chicago: University of Chicago Press, 1975), James M. Gustafson examines ways in which ethics, as a reflection on moral concerns, may be said to be a Christian project. Reinhold Niebuhr's *An Interpretation of Christian Ethics* (New York: Meridian Books, 1956) builds an excellent bridge between the theoretical concerns of this chapter and the kind of thinking examined in Chapter 7.

William James's *Essays on Faith and Morals*, edited by Ralph Barton Perry (New York: The New American Library, Inc., 1962) and his *The Varieties of Religious Experience* (New York: Macmillan Publishing Company, Inc., 1961) present his explicitly religious thinking. Readers may consult Bruce W. Wilshire's edition of *William James: The Essential Writings* (New York: Harper and Row, 1971) to begin examining additional aspects of James's thought. The classic source for the study of William James is Ralph Barton Perry's two-volume work, *The Thought and Character of William James* (Boston: Little, Brown, & Company, 1935). Gay Wilson Allen's *William James: A Biography* (New York: The Viking Press, 1967) is as fine a single-volume study of James's life and thought as Bruce Kuklick's *The Rise of American Philosophy: Cambridge, Massachusetts, 1860-1930* (New Haven: Yale University Press, 1977) is of James's intellectual world. The chapter on James in William a. Clebsch's *American Religious Thought: A History* (Chicago: University of Chicago Press, 1973) situates James in the tradition of Edwards and Emerson.

Walter Rauschenbusch's most accessible books are *Christianity and the*

Social Crisis (New York: Harper & Row, 1964) and *A Theology for the Social Gospel* (Nashville: Abingdon Press, 1945). Ronald C. White, Jr., and C. Howard Hopkins place Rauschenbusch in relation to others who helped lead his movement in *The Social Gospel: Religion and Reform in Changing America* (Philadelphia: Temple University Press, 1976), as does the volume in the Library of Protestant Thought edited by Robert T. Handy, *The Social Gospel in America, 1870-1920: Gladden, Ely, Rauschenbusch* (New York: Oxford University Press, 1966).

As general studies of the role of religion in this period, I recommend:

Bowden, Henry W. *Church History in the Age of Science.* Chapel Hill: University of North Carolina Press, 1971.

Carter, Paul A. *The Decline and Revival of the Social Gospel.* Hamden, Conn.: Archon Books, 1971.

_____. *The Spiritual Crisis of the Gilded Age.* DeKalb: Northern Illinois University Press, 1972.

Howe, Daniel Walker, ed. *Victorian America.* Philadelphia: University of Pennsylvania Press, 1976.

Marty, Martin E. *Righteous Empire: The Protestant Experience in America.* New York: The Dial Press, 1970. Pp. 132-220.

Mead, Sidney E. *The Lively Experiment: The Shaping of Christianity in America.* New York: Harper & Row, 1963. Pp. 134-87.

CHAPTER 7

While there are almost as many definitions of theology as there are theologians, the reader who wants a concise, workable introduction to the theoretical perspective of this chapter may begin with two articles by Schubert M. Ogden, "What is Theology?" *The Journal of Religion* 52, no. 1 (January 1972): 22-40, and "Theology and Religious Studies: Their Difference and the Difference It Makes," *Journal of the American Academy of Religion* 44, no. 1 (March 1978): 3-17. Daniel Day Williams provides a helpful survey of the concerns of modern theology in *What Present-Day Theologians Are Thinking* (New York: Harper & Row, 1967).

The work of the two Niebuhrs has been instrumental in defining the task of modern theology, and there is no substitute for reading their major writings, preferably in chronological order.

Niebuhr, Reinhold. *Moral Man and Immoral Society: A Study in Ethics and Politics.* New York: Charles Scribner's Sons, 1932.

_____. *The Nature and Destiny of Man: A Christian Interpretation.*

Two volumes in one. Vol. 1, *Human Nature*. Vol. 2, *Human Destiny*. New York: Charles Scribner's Sons, 1953.

_____. *The Self and the Dramas of History*. New York: Charles Scribner's Sons, 1957.

Niebuhr, H. Richard. *The Social Sources of Denominationalism*. New York: Henry Holt and Company, Inc., 1929.

_____. *The Kingdom of God in America*. New York: Harper & Row, 1937.

_____. *The Meaning of Revelation*. New York: The Macmillan Company, Inc., 1941.

_____. *Christ and Culture*. New York: Harper & Row, 1951.

_____. *Radical Monotheism and Western Culture, with Supplementary Essays*. New York: Harper & Row, 1961.

_____. *The Responsible Self: An Essay in Christian Moral Philosophy*. New York: Harper & Row, 1963.

Excellent selected bibliographies of works by and about the two Niebuhrs may be found in:

Kliever, Lonnie. *H. Richard Niebuhr*. Waco: Word Press, 1977.

Patterson, Bob E. *Reinhold Niebuhr*. Waco: Word Press, 1977.

Nathan A. Scott, Jr.'s *Reinhold Niebuhr* (Minneapolis: University of Minnesota Press, 1963) gives a brief overview of Reinhold Niebuhr's life and works. And the essays in the special issue of *The Journal of Religion* 54, no. 4 (October 1974), interpret his theology from a variety of perspectives.

CHAPTER 8

As seen in note 3 in the text, definitions of modernization are legion. Peter Berger's *The Homeless Mind: Modernization and Consciousness* (New York: Random House, 1973) provides a relatively succinct, useful introduction. Richard D. Brown's *Modernization: The Transformation of American Life, 1600-1865* (New York: Hill and Wang, 1976) is an attempt to interpret an earlier period of American history in terms of modernization theory. Thomas Luckmann's *The Invisible Religion: The Problem of Religion in Modern Society* (New York: The Macmillan Company, Inc., 1967) focuses more precisely on how modernization affects religious experience.

Paul M. Harrison's *Authority and Power in the Free Church Tradition: A Social Case Study of the American Baptist Convention* (Carbondale: Southern Illinois University Press, 1959) is a model for the analysis of church organizations. The issues Harrison's study confronts within this particular denomination are surveyed more generally in Gibson Winter's *Religious Identity: The Formal Organization and Informal Power Structure of the Major Faiths in the United States Today* (New York: The Macmillan Company, Inc., 1968).

For the purposes of this chapter, to see the message of Martin Luther King in terms of the modernization of American society, readers may want to begin with Dr. King's *Where Do We Go From Here: Chaos or Community?* (New York: Bantam Books, 1967) and then study his life and works in David L. Lewis's *King: A Critical Biography* (Baltimore: Praeger, 1970). Dr. King's message might then be situated historically in the context provided by Joseph R. Washington, Jr.'s *Black Religion: The Negro and Christianity in the United States* (Boston: Beacon Press, 1964).

The basic themes of the "death of God" theology are expressed forthrightly in Thomas J. J. Altizer and William Hamilton's *Radical Theology and the Death of God* (Indianapolis: The Bobbs-Merrill Company, Inc., 1966). And Part One of Langdon Gilkey's *Naming the Whirlwind: The Renewal of God-Language* (Indianapolis: The Bobbs-Merrill Company, Inc., 1969) provides a useful critique and places the "death of God" movement in the intellectual and cultural context of modern theology.

CHAPTER 9

The basic theoretical perspective for this chapter is provided by Anthony F. C. Wallace in "Revitalization Movements," *American Anthropologist* 58 (1956): 264-81. Also useful in this regard is the article by Luther P. Gerlach and Virginia Hine, "Five Factors Crucial to the Growth and Spread of a Modern Religious Movement," *Journal for the Scientific Study of Religion* (Spring 1968), pp. 23-40.

Views of American society as ripe for or in need of revitalization are given in Robert N. Bellah's *The Broken Covenant: American Civil Religion in Time of Trial* (New York: The Seabury Press, 1975); Robert Nisbet's *Twilight of Authority* (New York: Oxford University Press, 1975); and Daniel Bell's *The Cultural Contradictions of Capitalism* (New York: Basic Books Inc., 1976).

Readers seeking an introduction to the variety of "new" religions in contemporary America may consult:

Ellwood, Robert S., Jr. *Religious and Spiritual Groups in Modern America.* Englewood Cliffs: Prentice-Hall, Inc., 1973.
Glock, Charles Y., and Bellah, Robert N., eds. *The New Religious Consciousness.* Berkeley: University of California Press, 1976.

Needleman, Jacob. *The New Religions*. Garden City: Doubleday & Company, Inc., 1970.

Wuthnow, Robert. *The Consciousness Reformation*. Berkeley: University of California Press, 1976.

Zaretsky, Irving I.; and Leone, Mark P., eds. *Religious Movements in Contemporary America*. Princeton: Princeton University Press, 1974.

Readers seeking to interpret the rise of charismatic and evangelical Christian churches should see:

Kelley, Dean M. *Why Conservative Churches Are Growing: A St dy in the Sociology of Religion*. New York: Harper & Row, 1972.

Hamilton, Michael P., ed. *The Charismatic Movement*. Grand Rapids: William B. Eerdmans Publishing Company, 1975.

Quebedeaux, Richard. *The Young Evangelicals: Revolution in Orthodoxy*. New York: Harper & Row, 1974.

_____. *The New Charismatics: The Origins, Development, and Significance of Neo-Pentecostalism*. Garden City: Doubleday & Company, Inc., 1976.

_____. *The Worldly Evangelicals*. San Francisco: Harper & Row, 1978.

For an introduction to thinking about the significance of pluralism for the understanding of religion, see the essays edited by F. Stanley Lusby and Charles H. Reynolds as "Dilemmas of Pluralism: The Case of Religion in Modernity," a special issue of *Soundings* 61, no. 3 (Fall 1978).

EPILOGUE

As resources for developing a way of thinking about religion that embraces both substantive and functional concerns, readers should see Clifford Geertz's "Religion as a Cultural System" and Melford E. Spiro's "Religion: Problems of Definition and Explanation," both of which are included among the essays edited by Michael Banton as *Anthropological Approaches to the Study of Religion* (London: Tavistock Publications, 1966). In this respect, the two appendices of Peter L. Berger's *The Sacred Canopy: Elements of a Sociological Theory of Religion* (Garden City: Doubleday & Company, Inc., 1967) are also valuable.

INDEX

About the Author

JAMES G. MOSELEY is Associate Professor of Religion and Chairman of the Division of the Humanities at New College of the University of South Florida in Sarasota. He is the author of *A Complex Inheritance: The Idea of Self-Transcendence in the Theology of Henry James, Senior, and the Novels of Henry James.*